Another volume, —
another token of my
fondest love.

Sept. 3rd 1903.

The Master Musicians

EDITED BY
FREDERICK J. CROWEST

Schumann

a

Robert Schumann

Schumann

By

Annie W. Patterson

Mus. Doc., B.A.

(Royal University of Ireland)

Author of *The Story of Oratorio*, Etc.

With

Illustrations and Portraits

London: J. M. Dent & Co.

New York: E. P. Dutton & Co.

1903

INSCRIBED

WITH MUCH ESTEEM

TO THE COMPOSER'S YOUNGEST DAUGHTER

FRÄULEIN EUGENIE SCHUMANN

Preface

SCHUMANN, as editor, essayist and composer, occupies a unique and striking position. His early literary culture and poetic tendencies, as his subsequent work in connection with the *Neue Zeitschrift für Musik*, rendered him a man of many parts. Thus it happens that, if we consider him from his many aspects of endeavour, he appeals to a wider art circle than that which is bounded within the pale of Music alone. Yet, in the realm proper of music, after a very limited period of healthful activity, Schumann left behind him specimens of well-nigh every form of classical composition, in all of which he attained to a high and rare artistic standard of originality and excellence.

So great, indeed, were Schumann's claims upon the public for recognition as a musician that, whereas more than one admirable biography exists of the composer, narrators scarcely penetrate beyond historical data and critical notices of his works, leaving the man—as he appears in his essays and letters—but partially known to us. We have it upon the authority of Madame Clara Schumann herself that, particularly from his private correspondence, it is easiest to arrive at a just estimate of the sterling personal traits of her husband.[1] Hence the writer, in the present instance, while

[1] See page 141.

not neglecting a life narrative and necessarily brief survey of musicianship, has endeavoured, as far as was possible, by an analysis of his correspondence, to let the great tone poet speak to the readers through his own thoughts and mental aspects as displayed so vividly in his various writings and letters. Thereby it is hoped to supply that which has hitherto been wanting in the way of an accurate character sketch.

For biographical details the authoress wishes to express her special indebtedness to Wasielewski's *Life of Schumann*, an able work, which Spitta places first in the list of Schumann authorities; Reissmann's *Life of Schumann* (English translation by A. L. Alger), which contains much valuable information and critical material; and, notably, to Spitta's scholarly and sympathetic sketch of Schumann in Grove's *Dictionary of Music and Musicians*. Other interesting works, dealing with the musician and his output, will be found catalogued in the Bibliography (Appendix B), from which it will be seen that there is no lack of valuable Schumann literature.

In presenting Schumann's personality, the writer has sought, as has already been implied, by a careful and thorough analysis of his essays and correspondence, to comply with the wish of his late distinguished wife that the man himself should be allowed speech through his writings, and especially his letters. For this purpose frequent references have been made to the published collections known as *Robert Schumann's Jugend Briefe* (with preface by Madame Clara Schumann), *Robert Schumann's Briefe* (compiled and edited by F. G. Jansen), and what private (unpublished) correspondence the authoress has been privileged to see and quote from through the courtesy of friends. Short extracts from the published letters have been taken from the excellent English translations by May Herbert of the above collections, known respectively as *Early Letters of Robert Schumann*, and *The Life of Robert Schumann told in His Letters*, to a perusal of which, in their entirety, the reader is earnestly recommended. Regarding Schumann as editor and essayist, space limitations in this case have precluded much in the way of quotation, especially as, apart from context, it is unfair to an author not to "hear him out," and from all sides of the question. But acknowledgment for the subject-matter dealt with is herewith made to Fanny Raymond Ritter's apt translation into English of *Gesammelte Schriften über Musik und Musiker*, edited by Schumann himself, and popularly known as *Music and Musicians*.

Above all, the writer must not omit to mention F. G. Jansen's exhaustive and highly-interesting book, *Die Davidsbündler, aus Robert Schumann's Sturm und Drange Periode*. Professor Jansen ranks as one of the foremost of Schumann authorities; and for aid in translating extracts into English from his work in question, the warmest thanks are herewith tendered to Mrs Sophie Metcalfe. This lady, herself a talented pianist and professor of music, and a daughter of the late gifted pianist, Mrs Thomson (*née* Robena Laidlaw), has also most kindly permitted the publication, for the first time, of two interesting early letters of Schumann to her mother, which throw light upon the composition of that well-known pianoforte cycle, the

"Fantasiestücke" (Op. 12). To many other musical friends, and particularly to Mr A. J. Hipkins and Mr Algernon S. Rose — both foremost authorities on the pianoforte literature of the day—the authoress also desires to express her sincere thanks for much kind interest and valued help in collecting material for the present volume. Last, but not least, she feels honoured in being permitted to inscribe the book, with much esteem, to Fräulein Eugenie Schumann, the composer's youngest daughter, to whom she has had the privilege of a personal introduction, and who has rendered valuable help in suggesting appropriate illustrations, as well as by confirming the writer's opinion with regard to the lines upon which a just and sympathetic estimate of her distinguished father — both as artist and man — might be laid before the reader.

In conclusion, the biographer pleads the vastness and variety of the material at her disposal, if, at best, the multiple accomplishments of one of the most original of Master Musicians be touched upon in a light narrative, rather than deeply critical or erudite, fashion. The story in itself is more than interesting—it is deeply touching and instructive.

ANNIE W. PATTERSON.

LONDON, *February* 1903.

Contents

BIOGRAPHICAL

CHAPTER I

CHAPTER II

CHAPTER III

CHAPTER IV

Contents

CHAPTER V

CHAPTER VI

CHAPTER VII

THE MAN

CHAPTER VIII

CHAPTER IX

Contents

CHAPTER X

CHAPTER XI

CHAPTER XII

THE MUSICIAN AND WRITER

CHAPTER XIII

CHAPTER XIV

Contents

CHAPTER XV

CHAPTER XVI

CHAPTER XVII

CHAPTER XVIII

APPENDIX A

APPENDIX B

List of Illustrations

SCHUMANN

Biographical

CHAPTER I

Birth and Parentage—Inherited Characteristics—Early Musical Training—Hearing Moscheles play—Literary Culture—The Mystic Nonade—The Poetry Period—First Literary Attempts—Friendship with Rosen—First Year at Leipzig University—At Heidelberg under Thibaut—Music *versus* Law—His Mother's Letter to Wieck—A Peep into Wieck's House—Enthusiasm as a Pianist.

MUSIC is not hereditary, else we should scarcely speak of it as a "gift." The Bach family, the Mozarts—father and son—the Wesleys, and other noted instances of apparently inherited musicianship, are, doubtless, but the exceptions which prove the rule. We are now speaking of music as it displays itself in a Master Musician, in other words, of *musical genius*. Between talent and genius there is a wide gap. Talent flourishes under favourable circumstances and partakes, naturally, of the atmosphere in which it is reared. Genius—most often a martyr as far as environment is concerned—is born to over-ride obstacles and adversity, and to come to maturity in surroundings of its own creation. Beethoven's genius developed all the sooner, probably, owing to the early if severe musical discipline which he received; but in later years he chose his own path. Handel was a sturdy combatant from the first, and, by the power of his indomitable will, even in childhood, he carved his way to his heart's desire in spite of parental opposition. Schumann, the dreamer and romanticist, won his niche in Parnassus by the sheer devotion and poetry of his nature. If Handel's claim to immortality might be compared to the title of one of his last oratorios, "The Triumph of Time and Truth," then Schumann may be considered to have owed his victory to Love, the Conqueror.

Birth and Parentage

Robert Alexander Schumann was born at Zwickau, Saxony, on June 8, 1810, the exact hour of his birth being given by Wasielewski as 9.30 in the evening. His father, Friedrich August Gottlob Schumann, the son of a clergyman, appears to have been a man of no ordinary talent and culture. The elder Schumann had begun life humbly as a shop assistant. But he found time to improve himself in literature; and having been employed by one Heinse, a bookseller at Zeitz, he thereby won that experience in the book trade which enabled him later on to start, in conjunction with one of his brothers, the eminent publishing firm of Schumann Brothers. This event took place at Zwickau in 1808. Some thirteen years previously Friedrich August had married Johanna Christina, daughter of Herr Schnabel, the town physician of Zeitz. Madame Friedrich Schumann seems to have been a remarkable woman in many ways. She has been blamed for opposing her son Robert in his desire to make music his profession; and it was certainly out of respect to her wishes that he only entered upon his beloved calling after the first glow of youth was past. But

The Birthplace
Hauptmarkt
Zwickau

mother's love, strong, solicitous and maybe almost morbid in its anxiety for the boy's future prospects, surely covered her mistake. The musician himself was all along deeply conscious of this, and hence, out of filial duty, he came near sacrificing himself and his art. But such a calamitous happening was mercifully prevented. Love and genius, instead of opposing each other, made a compromise. But we are anticipating.

Inherited Characteristics

Robert was the youngest child. Usually the latest born is the most favoured and petted by parents and elder members of a family. The mother, especially, is tenderly drawn to the last baby—she would fain keep him a baby always. That much of Robert's romanticism, and that hyper-sensitiveness that amounted almost to melancholy, were owing to the influence of his mother's disposition, has been alleged. But the boy seems also to have inherited from his father that ardent determination to win his way at his chosen pursuits in spite of drawbacks; and so the morbid side of his temperament was generally fairly balanced by the enthusiasm and ambition of his artistic nature.

Early Musical Training

Neither of Schumann's parents were musical in the usually accepted meaning of the term. His father, however, seems to have favoured his son's love for music, and it is certain that he procured for Robert the best musical instruction that could be obtained in Zwickau. This included lessons from J. G. Kuntzsch,[1] the organist of the

[1] It is said that Kuntzsch, in later years, when Schumann had finally launched upon music as a profession, prophesied that his erst pupil would

Marienkirche, who appears to have been keenly struck with his young pupil's talent. How early the boy's gift displayed itself it is impossible to say. Writing to a distinguished amateur friend[1] in 1839, Schumann himself speaks of having begun to compose in his seventh year. At eleven we find him acting as accompanist at a performance of Schneider's "Weltgericht,"[2] when he is described as having stood at the piano throughout, his master, Kuntzsch, acting as conductor.[3] Shortly after this he is also accredited with having organised many home musical *réunions*, principally among young people of his own age, and to have gained quite a reputation in the social circles of his family as a clever extempore player. Thus early did the creative yearning make itself evident. Ere long Kuntzsch declared the boy could progress alone—in other words, the master felt that his pupil was outstripping him. So impressed was the elder Schumann with the musicianship of his son that at one time he made an effort to procure for him the tuition of C. M. von Weber, who had, some short time previously (1817), been elected Capellmeister in Dresden. Weber was willing to undertake the training of the boy—then only eight years old—but, for some unexplained reason, the project fell through.

This circumstance serves to show that Robert's father may have taken more interest and pride in the musical

attain to the highest fame. Schumann appears to have highly esteemed his first pianoforte teacher, and, in 1845, dedicated to Kuntzsch the "Studies for Pedal Piano," Op. 56.

[1] M. Simonin de Sire (of Dinant),

[2] Oratorio by F. Schneider (1786-1853).

[3] Spitta in *Dictionary of Music and Musicians* (Grove).

tendencies of his little boy than is generally supposed. A year later the parent again indirectly gave the young musician that very impetus towards musical study which his probably dormant inclination required. He took the lad to hear Ignace Moscheles play at Carlsbad. How deeply the child was impressed was proved by after occurrences. During the whole of his career the composer cherished the highest reverence for the famous friend of Mendelssohn, and some of his earlier works—perhaps notably the Pianoforte Variations on the name "Abegg" (Op. 1)—show the influence of the great pianist's technique. Again, in a letter to Moscheles, dated 20th November 1851, Schumann tells the elder musician how, thirty years before, he had preserved "as a sacred relic" a programme which the virtuoso had handled.[1] Undoubtedly the hearing Moscheles play was a landmark in the career of Robert Schumann. He was then about nine years old.

Hearing Moscheles

Now followed a period in the youth's life which may be described as more literary than musical, though music was never quite forgotten. At ten the boy was sent to the local school of his own town, through the various classes of which he passed, leaving in Easter 1828. On March 29 of this year he matriculated at the University of Leipzig as a law student. This step was taken to gratify his mother. The young man, now in his eighteenth year, longed to

Literary Culture

[1] In later years the respect of both musicians seems to have been mutual for each other. Moscheles' "Piano and 'Cello Sonata" (Op. 121) is dedicated to Schumann.

follow the art to which he was so devoted, and he had little or no taste for jurisprudence. But his father, who had been inclined to foster his youngest son's musical tastes, had died in 1826, and his mother's wish that he should be a lawyer seemed so urgent that the sense of filial duty carried the day.

Mystic Nonades

There are few life histories of celebrities which, if analysed, do not present epochs of thought and activity in some one direction which, more or less, colour after achievements. That these epochs should serve as periods of progress we willingly allow. That the mind should work in a regular time-cycle, passing from one phase of sentiment to another with almost mathematical exactness, is a metaphysical mystery scarcely as yet explored. Nature is supposed to renew or rehabilitate the physical frame every seven years; perhaps a turning-point in mental development may be reached—especially in emotional or poetical subjects—every ninth year, *nine* being the mystic number, the three times three of the seer. Be this as it may, the sequence of numbers, which strangely influence the institutions of man as the universe of the Creator, may affect the lives, and especially the mental growth, of human beings more than people think. It is certainly curious that Schumann's adolescence, or development period, may be roughly classed into two divisions of nine years each. His first nonade witnessed his childhood's musical aspirations and early triumphs in composition—that branch of art in which he was destined, in later years, to win his laurels. His maturer work periods might also be relegated to nonades.

The second nine, from his tenth to eighteenth year, marked an undoubted divergence of interest. During this time, partly owing to scholastic discipline and also due to inclination towards general culture derived from his father, we find the future composer much attracted by the Muse of Poetry. The shop of Schumann Brothers was a storehouse of treasures to the lad; and we may be sure that, in his thirst for book knowledge, Robert was, at this period of his life, enthusiastically aided and encouraged by both his parents. Romantic literature, and especially emotional verse, attracted him most. Among his favourite authors Spitta[1] quotes Schulze, the author of *Die Bezauberte Rose* ("The Enchanted Rose"); Franz van Sonnenberg, who afterwards went insane; Byron; and, notably, Jean Paul Richter.

Poetry Period

The influence of these writers, and especially that of the last-named, Jean Paul, upon the susceptible, keenly imaginative and somewhat sentimental mind of the lad Schumann, was apparently very great. His admiration for Jean Paul, whose writings he first came across in his seventeenth year, never wavered during his life. He frequently refers to the poet in his letters; and when, some years later, he visited Bayreuth on a holiday trip, the musician called upon Jean Paul's widow and obtained from her, as a valued memento, a portrait of his favourite bard. Nor was Schumann a reader only, but, in these days of his teens, he aspired also to be a writer of verses. Some of

First Literary Attempts

[1] *Dictionary of Music and Musicians* (Grove).

these poems he subsequently (in 1827) set to music. He must early have displayed facility with his pen, for at fourteen years of age we find him one of the contributors to a series, published by his father, entitled *Bildergallerie der beruhmtesten Menschen aller Völker und Zeiten* ("Portrait Gallery of the Most Famous Men of all Nations and Times"). Thus was doubtless sown the seed of that facility in putting his thoughts to paper so characteristic of Schumann the letter-writer, editor and essayist.

Friendship with Rosen

The commencement of his university career was pleasantly marked by his making the acquaintance of a fellow-student, Gisbert Rosen, for whom he conceived a fast and devoted friendship. Young Rosen had decided to study at Heidelberg, and thither Schumann accompanied him on a short pleasure trip before settling down to his own course at Leipzig, from which town he frequently wrote to his friend. During the first few months of his university work Schumann grew low-spirited, as would appear from those letters, and from others (to his mother) belonging to this time. Always of a retiring disposition, he preferred to keep to himself, finding little that was congenial to his refined and sensitive nature in the students' club. It speaks much for the sympathetic and congenial nature of young Rosen that he should have succeeded in winning the confidence of the reserved youth Robert, who hitherto had been accustomed only to the society of the women of his family, and communion with his books. That he experienced the greatest difficulty in making up his mind to regularly commence his selected course of study, seems evident. He confesses, in one of his letters to his friend, that his first half-year was mainly spent in playing the piano, writing letters and "Jean Pauliads."

First Year at Leipzig University

After a little he seems to have come somewhat out of his shell and to have mixed in congenial society. He was a frequent guest at the house of Professor Carus, whose accomplished wife gathered round her a rare musical and artistic circle. Among interesting people met at these *réunions* was Marschner,[1] and notably Friedrich Wieck, who was destined to be our hero's future father-in-law. That music, rather than either law or literature, was very strongly in the mind of Schumann at the time, there can be little doubt. The early death of Schubert had just taken place (1828). This sad circumstance seems to have keenly affected Robert Schumann; and, with a band of fellow musical students, he devoted special attention to the works —only too little known then—of the greatest of song-writers. J. S. Bach was another composer whom he regarded now, as indeed always, with an admiration and respect akin to worship. To some it might appear curious that the music of the earnest and scholarly old Cantor of the Thomas Schule, Leipzig, and the spontaneous melody of Schubert, as the fanciful writings of Jean Paul, should all have appealed to the mind of Schumann. Apparently the mental characteristics of the two musicians named, as of the romanticist, were as opposite in tendency as could well be imagined. But Schumann had a great deal of the philosopher about him, and he peered beneath the surface

[1] Heinrich Marschner, German opera composer (1796-1861).

of scholasticism as of sentimentality. Bach bears analysis; in fact, only after the most careful and sympathetic study does one find, under counterpoint and fugue, that staunch nobility and resoluteness of aim and purpose which never fail to stir the soul to loftiest thought and endeavour. If anything can, this attraction which creative minds of a heroic and fanciful cast exercised over Schumann shows the many-sidedness of his own disposition, both as a dreamer and thinker. It is also worthy of note that, although he was lax in attending legal lectures at the university, he was much interested in the philosophic classes of Krug, and appears at the time to have delved deeply into the works of Kant, Schelling and others.

At Heidelberg under Thibaut

In 1829 Schumann joined his friend Rosen at the University of Heidelberg, where, doubtless, the presence of the famous teacher, A. F. J. Thibaut[1]—who combined a love for music with the severer pursuit of the law—was an attraction to both young men. It does not appear, however, that, in Schumann's case, professor and student got beyond the formalities of a college intimacy, though, later, we find Thibaut strongly encouraging Schumann in his desire to relinquish law for music. No wonder that even his master should so counsel him; for, as in Leipzig, so in Heidelberg, his beloved piano claimed almost all the young student's attention. While in Heidelberg he practised seven hours a day, and those who then heard him play speak in the highest terms of his technique and

[1] Author of *Ueber Rheinheit der Tonkunst* ("On Purity in Musical Art.")

execution. It is worthy of note that his first—and, indeed, only—public appearance as a pianist was made here at this time, when he again showed his appreciation for Moscheles by playing that master's Variations on the "Alexander-Marsch," and made quite a sensation. Pressed often afterwards to play again at concerts and various musical entertainments, he invariably refused.

Music versus *Law*

On the whole, Schumann appears to have been much happier in Heidelberg than in Leipzig. The restraints of university life seem to have been very slight, and surroundings were more congenial. That the youth spent more time over amusement than study also appears evident. His letters at this period to his guardian, Herr Rudel, requesting for increases to his allowance, make amusing reading. "You would immensely favour me, most esteemed Herr Rudel," he writes on one occasion, "if you would let me have as much money as you can as soon as you can."[1] At another time, when he desires to travel to Italy, he speaks comically of being obliged to make the journey some time, so that it would make no difference if he used the money for the purpose then or subsequently. Indeed, pleasure trips at the time seem frequent; and it was during this very sojourn in Italy that he first heard, and was deeply impressed by, the marvellous playing of Paganini. It was only during his third year in the artistic town of Heidelberg that Schumann seems to have braced himself up to make a last attempt to interest himself in his legal studies. He took what was called a

[1] Early Letter.

Repetition Course with an old lawyer; and, occasionally, it would seem from his home letters that his mind was at last being won over to the profession which his fond mother had designed for him. But Nature would not be thus outraged. The musician's entire want of appreciation of Jurisprudence appeared only too evident upon closer acquaintance with the subject, and at last Madame Schumann was persuaded to leave the decision of her son Robert's future career to the judgment of that eminent teacher of the pianoforte, Friedrich Wieck, with whose family Schumann was afterwards to be so closely associated.

His Mother's Letter to Wieck

It is from a letter of hers to Wieck, written at this crisis in her son's life, that we really get an insight into the true devotion and solicitude of the mother for her youngest and highly-gifted child. Instead of this representing her as being a hard and determined woman, whose personal ambition for her offspring would allow her to over-rule even his own happiness and healthful exertion, we see therein the anxiety of mother-love, as also the earnest desire that her son's future success should be assured before any definite step was taken. An extract from this interesting epistle[1] may here be quoted:—

"I know that you love music—do not let that feeling plead for Robert, but consider his age, his means, his strength and his future. I beg, I implore you, as a husband, a father, and the friend of my son, act like an

[1] Quoted in its entirety in Wasielewski's *Life of Schumann*. *See* also Reissmann's *Life* (Translated by A. L. Alger).

honest man, and give me your plain, frank opinion—let me know what he has to fear or to hope."

Old Wieck must have been touched with the fervour of the appeal in this letter, and probably he fully realised the responsibility cast upon him in making him arbitrator in such a case. His reply was to the effect that a final decision could only lie with Robert himself, if he felt sure of his powers. At all events, music carried the day; and, with newly-awakened ambitions and aspirations we may be sure, Schumann found himself once again at Leipzig, under the immediate tuition of Wieck himself, in whose house he was for some time a resident student. This was in the year 1830. Clara, Wieck's gifted daughter, was then but a little girl of eleven. Schumann was twenty.

Peep into Wieck's House

Alfred Dörffel, the pianist, gives us a pleasant little peep into the abode of Wieck, which, although the period is a few years later,[1] gives us an idea of homeliness and simplicity which is pleasing. The Wiecks were giving a concert and Dörffel wished to go. At the time he was but a small boy, and had no money. Upon the advice of his master he called upon old Wieck and begged for a ticket, saying he was learning Schumann's "Papillons," which Clara Wieck was to play at the concert. "Show me your hands," said Wieck to the tiny lad, who could barely stretch a seventh. Eventually, much amused, Wieck got the embryo pianist to play the piece, which he did manfully, though the piano stool was far too low for him. However, the child had the knack of playing

[1] 1835.

octaves as if broken (in *arpeggio*), but very quickly, and he took the "Papillons" at a brisk pace. Wieck roared with laughter, while a young girl (Clara) and a young man (Schumann), who were standing together at the window listening, appeared to enjoy all immensely. "Good," said Wieck, when the brave little performer had finished. "Come to the orchestra; you want no ticket." Consequently, young Dörffel was admitted that evening, and, finding a place near Clara, was in ecstasies of delight.[1]

Enthusiasm as a Pianist

Such was "Father Wieck," under whom Schumann now began to pursue his pianoforte studies with intense ardour and energy. The young musician's first aim seems to have been, naturally, to perfect himself as an executive artist. To this end he worked assiduously at wrist and finger exercises, and rather shirked the study of harmony, which Wieck considered he ought to combine with his daily technical drill. The fact was that, as is often the case with most great creative minds, Schumann had a disinclination to assimilate dogma in the usual humdrum fashion, and must have early formulated his own rules of composition, reading between the lines, and following the spirit rather than the letter of cut-and-dry theory. From the circumstance that Schumann sought to perfect himself first as a performer, it has been suggested that, at the commencement of his studies with Wieck, he was not quite certain of his powers as a composer. But as the "Toccata" had been commenced (according to his own statement in a letter) in 1829, and there seems reason to believe that the Variations on the name

[1] Narrated in Jansen's *Die Davidsbündler*.

"Abegg" and the "Papillons" were also written about this time, it seems more likely that, while under Wieck, he was simply putting forth his best energies as an executant, not unlikely spurred on to excel in this department by the remarkable talent already displayed as a performer by the youthful Clara Wieck.

CHAPTER II

A Fortunate Calamity—From Piano to Composition—Early Impressions of Clara Wieck—Musical and Social Life at Leipzig—The Origin of the *Neue Zeitschrift*—Its Nature and *Raison d'être*—The "Davidsbündler"—The Musician as Editor—The Writer as Composer—Admiration of Mendelssohn—Mendelssohn's Attitude to Schumann—Different Traits of the Two Musicians.

ACCIDENT and adversity are often spoken of as blessings in disguise. In the case of Schumann the calamity, or experiment, rather, which led to his maiming his hand, and so effectively putting a stop to his career as a virtuoso, must be regarded as a fortunate one. The way it happened was as follows: Schumann, to facilitate the rapid acquirement of perfect freedom of finger action, used a device whereby the third finger was drawn back and prevented from moving while the other fingers played. This contrivance, if it had not been carried to the point of overstraining, might perhaps have effected its purpose and produced greater agility of finger. But the pianist, anxious to make up for the lost time of his first youth, wherein the hand is best made naturally nimble, overdid the experiment and permanently maimed his finger. Thus was an executant baulked on the very threshold of his career. But thus also

Fortunate Calamity

was an emotional tone poet turned perforce to that very channel of output in which he could find most congenial scope for expressiveness of the wondrous thoughts which burned within him.

From Piano to Composition

On Professor Jansen's authority we learn that Dr Otto of Schneeberg tried to cure the injury to Schumann's finger by electricity, but the weakness—the result of overstraining—could not be eradicated. This put an end, not only to the young musician's pianoforte studies under Wieck, but also to a contemplated course which he had hoped to take with Hummel. Writing to Töpken in 1833, he refers casually to the accident: "I still play the piano very little," he says, "as I have a lamed finger on my right hand. Through a trifling damage and subsequent carelessness the injury has become so serious that I can hardly play with the whole hand."[1] That the musician deeply felt the calamity that had befallen him we can scarcely doubt. Yet it is characteristic of his eminently philosophic spirit that, having parted company with one aim in life, he immediately turned his attention to another branch of musicianship—that one in which he was destined to shine so conspicuously—composition. His pianoforte lessons having been brought to an abrupt conclusion, he now determined to perfect himself in the theoretical part of creative work, and, for this purpose, placed himself under the instruction of Capellmeister Dorn,[2] then a notable figure in the musical

[1] *Die Davidsbündler* (Jansen).

[2] Heinrich Dorn (1804-1892), conductor and composer, was highly respected as Capellmeister at Leipzig, Cologne and Berlin.

world of Leipzig. That Schumann worked for his new master in anything like a conventional or methodical way was scarcely to be expected of one of his exceptional temperament. He had already imbibed the leading principles of form and construction; he utilised these now as mere skeletons around which to wreathe the wealth of his poetic fancy, probably often to the astonishment of his preceptor. But Dorn speedily recognised the rare talents of his gifted pupil; and though he protested against too much "free" work, yet he thought very highly of the young musician. Schumann himself afterwards expressed his indebtedness to Dorn's instructions, averring that he had learnt more from his teaching than Dorn could believe.

The winter of 1832-1833 was spent principally at his home in Zwickau and with his brothers at Schneeberg. A Symphony in G belongs to this period; but, as it was never published, the composer probably considered it an immature work, and simply as the outcome of his student period under Dorn. It was, however, performed at Zwickau (Nov. 18, 1832); and this occasion, apart from the rendering of the Symphony in itself, was perhaps a significant happening in the life of Schumann. The concert on this occasion was given by Clara Wieck, then thirteen years of age.

Early Impressions of Clara Wieck

When at her father's house, Schumann had doubtless had many opportunities of becoming acquainted with and marvelling at the wonderful executive talents of the young performer, who was one day to be his devoted helpmeet and the foremost exponent of his pianoforte works. But this was probably the first occasion upon which we can record any definite expression of his appreciation for the young pianist herself and her, even at that early age, brilliant powers as an executant. "Zwickau," he writes, "was enthusiastic for the first time in its life." He also characterises the young artist's rendition as "perfect." Thus was forged, perhaps, the first link in a chain of admiration, later on destined to develop into the most earnest devotion, for a woman whose talents and many excellent qualifications of character entitle her to rank among the foremost musical artists of her sex.[1]

Musical and Social Life at Leipzig

In 1833 Schumann was again in Leipzig. Unlike many of his fellow-artists, he had certain small private means of his own, so that the necessity of making a living out of his profession was not pressing; consequently we find him spending his time, for the most part, over his early compositions, or in the society of congenial friends. Among the latter was the charming Madame Henriette Voigt, for whom the composer cherished the highest respect and esteem and whom he afterwards corresponded with in terms of affectionate regard, making her a confidant in his love affairs. Henriette Voigt was an amateur pupil of L. Berger, and both she and her husband, Carl Voigt (a Leipzig merchant), entered with keen appreciation into the musical achievements of the day. That Madame Voigt thoroughly sympathised with the reserved, if strongly imaginative, temperament of Schumann is evidenced from a little incident. After a spell of some delightful music

[1] *See* page 118.

together, they went out for an hour's boating. During all this time Schumann observed a complete silence, which was unbroken by the lady. Upon making his adieux, the strangely reticent but deeply sensitive man exclaimed that never before had they understood each other so perfectly![1] Compositions of this time appear to have been an Impromptu for the piano on a Romanza by Clara Wieck,[2] who added composition to her executive attainments; the "Toccata" (Op. 7); and a second set of Studies for Piano, after Paganini's "Capriccios" (Op. 10), a first set having been written in 1832.

Origin of the Neue Zeitschrift

Another social influence of this time were the evening *réunions* held, with other enthusiastic musical young men, at a restaurant. These meetings, which extended from 1833 to 1834, were mainly given up to the discussion of musical topics of the day. The spirit of art reform was strong among the little *coterie*. Many were the subjects of their debates and conferences, but no themes appeared of such "burning" import as the decadence of music of the day—Rossini alone on the stage and Herz and Hünten at the pianoforte—and the weakness and servility of criticism, even in the *Allgemeine Musikalische Zeitung*, the principal musical journal of Leipzig, edited by Fink. To remedy these abuses it was proposed to start a musical paper which, with unbiassed honesty and independence, might bring about a better state of public opinion, as much with regard to music itself as to improve the status of its

[1] Spitta, *Dictionary of Music and Musicians* (Grove)
[2] Published August 1833 (Op. 5).

foremost makers and exponents. Thus originated the idea of the *Neue Zeitschrift für Musik*,[1] the first number of which was issued on April 3, 1834.

The literary talents and inventiveness of Schumann found congenial scope in the *Neue Zeitschrift*. From his poetic fancy he evolved and incorporated in the new journal his mythic Society of the Davidsbündler —an art confraternity which originated from, and existed only in, the brain of the musician-editor himself. Even in his early youth, spite of unmusical surroundings, Schumann seems to have always entertained the loftiest ideals in musical art. For sham, mediocrity, and the prosaicism of ordinary talent he had but little tolerance; yet so refined and hypersensitive was the nature of the man that, instead of attacking abuses fiercely and in a state of bitter hostility, he preferred to work reform in the most chivalrous and courteous spirit. Thus, without descending to personalities or recriminations, he sought ever to show "a better way" than overstep a moderated tact and tolerant judgment by self-assertiveness and fault-finding. With the exalted models of Bach and Beethoven before him, he knew that their works, at this time, scarcely got deserved recognition, owing to the paltry taste in musical matters brought about by the mere "display" methods and often charlatanism of ambitious self-seekers. As has been already mentioned, the early death of Schubert, before

Its Nature and Raison d'être

[1] Associated with Schumann in this undertaking were Friedrich Wieck, Ludwig Schunke (more a pianist than a *littérateur*) and Julius Knorr, an ex-philological student.

publishers or the world knew that a genius had, almost in vain, solicited a hearing, had deeply affected his sympathetic countryman, and instilled in Schumann's mind the urgent need for bettering the relations of composers with publishers as with *impressarii* and operatic managers. Several schemes of this kind, for the wide-spread benefit of his beloved art and its devotees, were, from time to time, much in the thoughts of Schumann; but none, save the paper, took anything like a practical or lasting shape.

Davidsbündler

It may be asked, What really was the Society of the Davidsbündler? The idea, a Scriptural one, found its origin in David, the divinely-favoured one, as opposed to the Philistine host of ignorance, apathy and superficiality with which all great and noble impulses have to make war. There was also, doubtless, in Schumann's mind, the contest of poetry in art as at righteous variance with the more prosaic and often mercantile aspect in which artists, unworthy of the name, regarded their calling. Under the title of Davidites, Schumann ranged his followers. Almost all his friends and fellow-workers are referred to by some one or other fanciful name; thus old Wieck was (sometimes) Master Raro, Mendelssohn was Felix Meritis, Clara was Chiara, and perhaps also Zilia (Cecilia), etc. Even many rising lights in the musical firmament, as was the case with Chopin and Berlioz, were brought into the ranks of the Davidsbündler. Schumann himself, as characteristic of the fire as the gentleness of his nature, figured respectively as Florestan and Eusebius. When any special abuse had to be warmly attacked or strong enthusiasm expressed, he wrote under the *nom de plume* of Florestan; while Eusebius ever qualified the impetuosity or severity of a judgment. The arbiter between the two was represented by the man of moderate, more philosophic views, Master Raro, an imaginary character, occasionally pointing to Wieck, but more often the ideal of the perfect critic and counsellor to whose standard of excellent and impartial judgment Schumann himself was ever striving. Only one endowed with such a keen sense as he had of poetic imagery could have thought out and effectively sustained such an idea. In fact, not only did Schumann speak through the mouths of all his creatures of the Davidsbündler, but he was the Davidsbündler himself from the several points of view of his large, liberal and imaginative mind.

Schumann as Editor

The good which an honest and authoritative paper like the *Neue Zeitschrift* did for the art which it supported can scarcely be too fully estimated. It arose at a time when, as Schumann and his coadjutors knew, musical criticism was at a very low ebb on the Continent. Even in musical Vienna, probably owing to press censorship, the only organ of recognised musical importance was the *Allgemeine Musikalische Anzeiger*,[1] and this was really more of a trade paper. Fink's paper in Leipzig was influenced more or less in its opinions by the tastes and fashion of the day. Schumann broke fresh ground with utter fearlessness and independence. He had a very perfect understanding with

[1] Published by Tobias Haslinger in connection with his own firm.

his helpers and contributors, who seem to have worked for him to the best of their abilities and upon the friendliest of terms. Schumann, who was at first associated with Wieck, Schunke and Knorr in the venture, became, in 1835, sole editor and proprietor, in which dual capacity he continued until 1844—strange to say, once more a period of nine years' activity in a particular groove! His expressions with regard to art, and opinions upon music in general and its exponents, are pungent, thoughtful, and of more than passing worth. Among notable achievements of the editor-musician was the first press recognition of the genius of Chopin, as also of Berlioz. Schumann s insight, as touch ing the works of his great predecessors, cannot fail to be of assistance to the intelligent reader. After his resignation in 1844 he only contributed one more article to the paper —and that a remarkable one—upon Brahms.

Writer and Composer

That, during this busy literary nonade, Schumann should have found time to write some of his most famous compositions, is little short of marvellous. To this period belong the F sharp minor Sonata (Op. 11), the famous "Fantasiestücke"(Op. 12), the F minor Sonata (Op. 14), as also the "Davidsbündler-tänze," "Novelletten," "Kinderscenen," "Kreisleriana," "Humoresken," etc., etc. Varied, and sometimes cold and hostile, were the opinions of contemporary critics and composers with regard to the most of these works. A few, however, recognised that, in the "Carnival" and other pieces, a new master of striking originality, and one who thoroughly understood the resources of the pianoforte keyboard, had arisen. Thus Grillparzer, the poet, favourably noticed two of the earlier pieces in the *Musikalische Zeitung* in 1832—an honour which Schumann very much appreciated. Liszt and Moscheles were always sympathetic admirers. Mendelssohn, however, although a personal friend—he and Schumann frequently dined together—was strangely silent upon the subject of Schumann's musicianship. That Mendelssohn should have failed to estimate the high artistic attainments of his contemporary, or rather have been so reticent in acknowledging them, is all the more inexplicable when we discover how enthusiastic Schumann was, both in his letters and criticisms, about his distinguished compeer.

Admiration of Mendelssohn

Thus, while in the many charming letters of Mendelssohn we look in vain for some appreciation of Schumann the musician, the epistolary fervour of Schumann with regard to his great fellow-artist is worthy of note. Writing to his sister-in-law, Thérèse Schumann, the editor of the *Neue Zeitschrift* refers to Mendelssohn as a man to whom he looked up as to a lofty summit. He even speaks of him as being "a perfect god."[1] Again, in a communication to Zuccalmaglio,[2] he mentions having shown this able writer's essay on "Erste Töne" (a contribution to the *Neue Zeitschrift*) to Mendelssohn, who seems to have been very pleased with what the critic had said therein. In this letter[3] Schumann speaks of Mendelssohn's

[1] Letter from Leipzig, April 1, 1836.

[2] A. W. von Zuccalmaglio, a friend and contributor to the *Neue Zeitschrift*.

[3] To Zuccalmaglio, January 31, 1837.

wonderful enthusiasm and describes his face as a marvellous one, as it were immortal. Therein he also refers to *St Paul* in glowing terms, as a work in which one exquisite thought is constantly succeeded by another. At a later date[1] he characterises Mendelssohn as *the first musician of the age.* Such strong admiration of Mendelssohn, the man and musician, was unquestionably the outcome of a sincere heart, as free from envy of a more fortunate brother artist as it was incapable of empty adulation or time-serving.

Mendelssohn's Attitude to Schumann

Mendelssohn's attitude with regard to Schumann—certainly a negative rather than a depreciative one—has been accounted for by Dr Spitta[2] in that Schumann's occupation as a newspaper critic was distasteful to the composer of "Elijah," and that he (Mendelssohn) could not reconcile the idea of a journalist and musician being united in the same personality. That, spite of his generous and unqualified admiration of his great contemporary, Schumann had heard, probably exaggerated by the idle gossip of well-meaning (?) mutual friends, certain reports that Mendelssohn was not altogether friendly disposed towards him, seems evident from a casual remark in an early letter to Clara Wieck in their courtship period. To her, from whom he concealed nothing, and to whom he was in the habit of pouring forth his heart in his correspondence, he wonders if it was true what people had said, that Mendelssohn was not *sincere* with him. He then

[1] Letter to Simonin de Sire, March 15, 1839.

[2] See the scholarly and exhaustive article by Spitta on "Schumann" in *Dictionary of Music and Musicians* (Grove).

speaks of his own high estimation of his brother artist, but adds that the reports referred to would put him on his guard not to throw away devotion upon one who, perchance, criticised him adversely behind his back.

Different Traits of the Two Musicians

How far there may have been foundation for the reports—whatever they were—which had reached Schumann's ears, it is difficult to say. The frank and genial disposition of Mendelssohn, as the generosity of his character, coupled to his almost daily intercourse with Schumann, scarcely allow us to think that he was in any way unjustly biassed against his distinguished fellow-musician. Perhaps the best way of explaining the situation is to remember how very opposite they were to each other in temperament as in methods of musical output, albeit both were so strongly tinged with the spirit of modern musical romanticism and colour. Even in personality they were diverse: Schumann was reserved and taciturn and did not shine in social converse, preferring letter-writing to speech whenever possible. Mendelssohn, with his wondrous charm of expression and magnetic personality—although also an adept at correspondence—was the pet and idol of society, never failing to fascinate whatever circle he moved in by his ingenious and bright manner and address. Added to this, the music of the two men is so diverse: the clear form, smooth harmonies and general symmetry of Mendelssohn's polyphony have little in common with the veiled mysticism and, at times, intense passion displayed in the daring tone combinations of Schumann. We have purposely made this digression in the biographical narrative of Schumann's life in order to emphasise the fact that his creative works won their way but slowly at first, even with those most competent to judge of their originality, intensity of feeling and colour, and artistic excellence.

CHAPTER III

Schumann in Love—Ernestine von Fricken—A Broken Engagement —"From Old Dreams to New"—The Love that lived—Early Love-letters—Clara Wieck as Composer—Parental Opposition—A Move to Vienna—The Paper and "Red Tape"—Devotion to Schubert—A Steel Pen—Composition in Vienna.

Schumann in Love

BESIDES the start of the paper and his early musical compositions, another matter occupied the mind of Schumann in 1834. We have referred to his friendship for the accomplished Madame Henriette Voigt and the musical society which he met at her house. That one of his romantic turn of mind should early become susceptible to the influence of charming and sympathetic womanhood was only to be expected. He had already dedicated his Opus 1 to a young lady named Abegg, whom he had met at a ball, though no sentiment beyond admiration is connected with the incident, as the maiden in question was beloved by one of his friends. Among old Wieck's pupils was a certain Ernestine von Fricken, and for her Schumann appears to have now cherished a warmer feeling. In the summer of 1834 he wrote a very interesting letter[1] to his

[1] Early letter to his mother, from Leipzig, July 2, 1834.

mother, in which he speaks of having lately met this young girl, and of being struck with the purity and innocence of her mind, and her devotion to the highest art ideals. Her rare talents as a musician are also referred to, and then Schumann confides in his mother that, were he to select a wife, his future choice would rest here. Strange to say, in the same letter he mentions the youthful Clara, who was then in Dresden, and he speaks of her genius becoming more and more evident, and of the remarkably able letters which she sometimes wrote to him.

Ernestine von Fricken

At the time it must be remembered that Clara Wieck, the noble and gifted woman who was afterwards his wife, was little more than a child. Of Ernestine von Fricken we only know that she was a talented pupil of Wieck, and an intimate friend of Madame Voigt, who, doubtless, gave the young people many chances of meeting and conversing with one another. For a time Schumann was very much in love. About the beginning of September 1834 he wrote to Madame Voigt in his impulsive way about crying over some words of Ernestine written on the margin of his correspondent's letter—evidently Madame Voigt was in the secret of their mutual attachment. In this letter he speaks of his unmeasurable love for Ernestine, as of his great friendship for Madame Voigt herself. The treasure he possessed, he said, consisted in "three names," *i.e.*, Henriette, Ernestine and Ludwig.[1]

Shortly about this time Schumann had become engaged to Ernestine von Fricken. But the betrothal was ter-

[1] Ludwig Schunke, the pianist.

minated by mutual consent in the following year. In how far the affections of either or both were seriously concerned it is impossible to say. It is pleasant, however, to record that, after their respective marriages, their friendship continued. Schumann dedicated his Book of Songs (Op. 31) to Frau Gräfin Ernestine von Zedtwitz, as she then was. The lady herself seems always to have preserved a kindly memory of Schumann. She died young. After her death there was found among her belongings the first volume of Herlossohn's *Damenconversationslexicon*. The title of the volume scarcely suggests what one would associate with a romantic memento! Yet the binding was very costly and elegant—pink satin with gilt edges—and the musical articles therein had been written by Schumann. It was probably, to the owner, the one link with the dead past of things that might have been.[1]

Broken Engagement

But a still more potent influence than that of the "child-like mind" of Ernestine von Fricken was commencing to sway young Schumann. In the very year of his engagement (1834) he had written a wonderful letter to Wieck's gifted young daughter, who was already making her name famous as a brilliant and successful pianist. In that letter he had spoken of "distance" being but an "extended vicinity." Thus could he talk to her every day—"in a gentler whisper even than usual"—and know

"*From Old Dreams to New*"

[1] F. G. Jansen (author of *Die Davidsbündler aus Robert Schumann's Sturm and Drange Periode*) mentions this incident in the published collection of Schumann's Letters (English translation by May Herbert in *Life of Robert Schumann told in His Letters*).

that he was understood. Then he tells her of all the plans he had made for their correspondence—how he would fill a balloon with "unwritten thoughts"—how he longed to catch butterflies and send them as his messengers to her, etc. Finally he speaks of the joy which the postillion's horn gives him. Apparently the post had just brought him a missive from the girl pianist. "That postillion with his horn sent me out of my old dreams into new ones."[1] From this it seems evident that something stronger than his first love was claiming the right to pre-eminence. Even absence and distance—Clara was then on tour—but strengthened the yearning of his soul for the sympathy of the one most akin to him. And thus, rather through spiritual communion than by personal intercourse, arose in the emotional musician's heart his life's strong devotion to Clara Wieck.

How this love grew and gradually became a glad reality to him, a glance through the letters of Schumann, written at this time, can best show. On August 28, 1835, we see how unmistakably his heart is with Clara.

Love that lived

He then writes to her of "an angel face" which he sees constantly before him who was the exact image of "a certain Clara" of his acquaintance. The letter ends with, "You know how fond I am of you, so good-bye, Robert Schumann." With Schumann's usual superstitions about lucky names and dates, he calls his correspondent's attention to the fact that he was writing to her on Goethe's birthday—doubtless, to his

[1] *See* this remarkable epistle in its entirety in *Early Letters of Robert Schumann.*"

mind, a lucky omen! It was only to be expected that such a lover should choose a propitious occasion upon which to express himself with final decision. Thus, on the Eve of St Valentine's Day (February 13, 1836), he penned a characteristic epistle while waiting for the Zwickau coach. The substance of this, which we quote from the English translation of May Herbert,[1] runs as follows:—

"I am quite clear about my heart. Perhaps your father will not refuse if I ask him for his blessing. Of course there is much to be thought of and arranged. But I put great trust in our guardian angel. Fate always intended us for one another. I have known that a long time, but my hopes were never strong enough to tell you and get your answer before."[2]

From this on, Clara, "that glorious girl," as he so often calls her, is the bright, particular star of Schumann's existence. In his many letters to her he discusses their future hopes, confides in her all his aspirations, retails bits of news in his daily life, talks of his own works, of the people he meets, and of his opinions upon men and things in general: in short, he looks upon his betrothed as if she were a part of himself—of his own soul. "If you only knew," he writes, "how I value your opinions, not only in Art, but in everything, and how your letters cheer me." His remarks to his *fiancée* concerning his compositions are

Early Love-Letters

[1] *Early Letters of Robert Schumann.* Translated from the German by May Herbert, with an Introduction by Mme. Clara Schumann.

[2] *Ibid.*

specially interesting. There are "bridal thoughts," he tells her, in the "Davidsbündlertänze" and the "Fantasiestücke," which he will explain to her some day. On another occasion he speaks of happiness and perfect solitude as being essential to successful composition. Referring to one of Clara's own criticisms, he appears to think she makes too little of the "Davidsbündlertänze." These he characterises as differing very much from the "Carnival"—as much as a face does from a mask. "They," he adds, meaning the "Davidsbündlertänze," "were written in happiness, and the others in toil and sorrow."[1]

Clara Wieck as Composer

Clara Wieck was not only a young pianist of rare and striking ability, but she had a facile gift as a composer.[2] Several pianoforte compositions of hers have been published, and they show excellent musicianship and accurate knowledge of the technique and capabilities of her instrument. Schumann, severe and just critic as he was, and lofty as was his standard of creative output, hails her, even in his own department, as a companion artist. He realises, he writes to her, that, from her Romanze, they were meant to be man and wife. All her ideas came as if from his own soul, even as he ascribed his musical inspiration to her.[3] On one occasion he had even suggested that they should publish some things under their two names, in order that generations might look upon them as truly one in heart and thought, and might not be able to distinguish the work of one from the other.[4] We see

[1] *Early Letters.*

[2] See also page 120.

[3] Letter from Leipzig, July 10, 1839.

[4] Letter, June 22, 1839.

here the enthusiasm of the lover, doubtless. At the same time it is to be remembered that Schumann was too genuine and conscientious to praise art work if it were not worthy, no matter how high might be his personal esteem.

Parental Opposition

As far as the lovers themselves were concerned in their devotion towards, and trust in, each other, the courtship of Robert Schumann and Clara Wieck seems to have been an ideal one. But they were destined to suffer much from parental opposition to the match, in the form of the persistent refusal of Clara's father, Friedrich Wieck, to give his sanction to their union. Probably the old man hoped for a still more ambitious match for his distinguished daughter; at all events, he disapproved of Schumann as a son-in-law until the latter was in a better position of wealth and recognition. It may be also that the *maestro* was somewhat displeased that the young people had settled it between them before he was aware of what was going on; for Schumann, writing to his friend, Dr A. Kahlert, speaks of himself and his *fiancée* having discussed matters and exchanged vows without the knowledge of Clara's father.[1] Time passed on, however, and "Papa Wieck" was still obdurate. Writing on the subject to his sister-in-law, Schumann speaks of the old man being much wrapped up in Clara and not wishing to part with her; yet, with his customary tolerance and charity, the lover upholds the action of the parent to a certain extent, allowing that it was quite true that they both should be making more money in order to live comfortably. But he looks for the

[1] Letter, March 1, 1836.

"blessing of Heaven" to bring all to a hoped-for and joyous ending. Clara he describes as being firm in not giving him up; and he applauds her great strength of character.[1] Later on[2] he writes to his brothers, Edward and Carl, in a more hopeful spirit as to a near solution of the difficulty, trusting that ere long Wieck would soften and that "one of the most glorious girls the world had ever seen" would be his. Then he begs his brothers to arrange his finances so that he may not appear "empty-handed" before Wieck.

A Move to Vienna

It was doubtless with a view to improve his own prospects and standing, as well as to increase the interests of the paper, that, about this time, he made an effort to establish the *Neue Zeitschrift* in Vienna. For this reason he moved thither in 1838. Schumann naturally hoped much from this venture; for he was fain to believe in the grand musical traditions of the Austrian capital, which had been the home of so many noted musicians, including Mozart, Haydn, Beethoven and Schubert. But although Schumann liked the city itself immensely, no doubt being largely attracted to it on account of its artistic prestige, he himself and his paper failed to get the appreciation there which they deserved. The people he seems, however, to have found very genial and musically inclined; and although deploring the want of public spirit and co-operation there, as well as the "petty cliques," he remarks that there was no want of good intentions among the musical residents themselves.[3]

[1] Letter, December 15, 1837. [2] From Leipzig, March 19, 1838.
[3] Letter to Clara Wieck, written from Vienna, 25th October 1838.

The opposition which Schumann and the *Neue Zeitschrift* met with in Vienna seemed, indeed, mainly owing to "red tape" and the strictures of the public censors. Staunch and honest criticism, he found, would be constantly under supervision in his columns. Yet there was urgent need in the city for a thoroughly authoritative musical paper, there being, at the time, none of real weight published there save the *Allgemeine musikalische Anzeiger* of Haslinger.[1] So Schumann struggled on bravely for a time, although the many delays and the obstacles placed in his path by the city officials must have been particularly galling to one of his sensitive and ardent nature. The fruitless battle lasted for over half a year. At length the editor-musician wrote to his friend Zuccalmaglio that both his paper and himself were "out of place" in Vienna.[2] He then speaks of returning, with renewed experiences and courage, to resume his work in Leipzig on the old lines. Thus the year 1839 found Schumann once more in his former surroundings. That he was keenly disappointed at his want of success in Vienna there can be little doubt. The prospect of his marriage with Clara now seemed further off than ever. It is even said that, upon leaving Vienna, he thought seriously of crossing the water to settle permanently in England. Perhaps the idea of making England his future home had occurred to him through his acquaintance with Sterndale Bennett, who was in Leipzig from 1837 to 1838.[3] In any case, the intention came to

The Paper and "Red Tape"

[1] See page 24.
[2] Letter to Zuccalmaglio from Vienna, March 10, 1839.
[3] Spitta.

nothing, for in 1839 we find him once more at work in Leipzig, as he had inferred he would be in his communication, just mentioned, to Zuccalmaglio.

Devotion to Schubert

But the sojourn in Vienna had not been without its interesting incidents. While there, Schumann met many distinguished and influential people; but nothing so enthralled him as the unearthing of several unpublished compositions of Schubert. This he had accomplished through a visit to Schubert's brother, whom, in a letter[1] to the noted firm of Leipzig music publishers, Messrs Breitkopf & Härtel, he describes as "a poor schoolmaster, entirely without means," with eight children to support and having only the manuscripts of his famous brother as a legacy. Among the works which Schumann thus happily discovered were Schubert's Masses and Symphonies. It was indeed owing to Schumann's introduction and warm recommendation that the Symphony in C was shortly afterwards published by Breitkopf & Härtel, and performed at Leipzig on March 21, 1839, under Mendelssohn's *bâton.* It is particularly praiseworthy of Schumann that at this particular time—personally a very trying and anxious one for him—he should have spared no pains to kindle an interest on behalf of a brother artist who had died so young and almost without honour in his own land. The first performance of the C major Symphony at the Gewandhaus Concerts, followed by a glowing and remarkable article on the event from Schumann in the *Neue Zeitschrift*, undoubtedly called erudite attention to this beautiful work

[1] January 6, 1839.

and added it to the list of musical art treasures. Schumann was also happily instrumental in obtaining liberal terms, from the Leipzig publishers named, on behalf of the needy schoolmaster and his large family, for the accepted manuscripts.

Another little episode—we may even so characterise it, for Schumann himself, with all the romantic superstition of his poet's nature, is greatly stirred by it—was the finding, upon visiting the graves of Beethoven and Schubert in the Vienna churchyard, of a *steel pen* on the last resting-place of the former! With this Schumann afterwards wrote his own B flat Symphony—as if to propitiate his creative muse—as also the critical notice of Schubert's C major Symphony, already referred to, after the Leipzig performance. Although it might more properly be spoken of when we come to discuss the characteristic traits of the man himself, yet, in passing, it may be noticed that this faculty which many great minds possess of treasuring "inconsidered trifles" with a history "for luck," as the observance of happy anniversaries, habits of commencing and finishing important tasks on "fortunate days," and so on, had a strong hold upon Schumann. We have already seen how he looked upon a programme which the hand of Moscheles had touched as a "sacred relic," preserving it for years. Similarly we perceive him, close upon his thirtieth birthday, clinging with reverent affection to, and using, as it were a potent charm, a little rusted pen that his fancy probably suggested *may* have been dropped by Schubert on Beethoven's grave. Such things staid folk

A Steel Pen

may criticise as childish and foolish. To scientists of the twentieth century, however, there is nothing past belief in the transference of an electric current from the animate to the inanimate, and *vice versâ*. The "bump of veneration" may yet be proved rational enough in its apparent vagaries.

Compositions in Vienna

Neither during, nor previous to, his editorial experiment in Vienna had Schumann, the composer, been idle. While in the Austrian metropolis he had written his "Faschingsschwank aus Wien" (Op. 26), in which he introduced, quite "under cover," the tune of the forbidden "Marseillaise"— probably, as Spitta aptly suggests, a playful hit of the composer's at the strict official surveillance of the city. In a highly interesting letter[1] to Simonin de Sire,[2] Schumann himself gives a table, in order, of his compositions up to date, stating that he had not published his very early efforts, commenced from his seventh year. This list commences with the "Toccata"—which, according to the composer, was started in 1829 but not finished until 1833—and concludes with the "Blumenstück," "Humoreske," and the commencement of a Concerto and a "great Romantic Sonata" (doubtless the "Faschingsschwank"), all of which Schumann allots to the latter part of his Viennese period, a whole group—including the "Novelletten," "Kinderscenen," "Kreisleriana" and "Arabesque"—being placed as belonging to the year 1838. Apparently never had the composer been busier. Of these he speaks of liking the "Kreisleriana"

[1] March 15, 1839.

[2] Simonin de Sire (of Dinant, Belgium) was an enthusiastic amateur admirer. He and Schumann wrote to each other, but they never appear to have met.

the most, the idea for his fantastic Kapellmeister Kreisler being found in a novel of E. T. A. Hoffmann.[1] This letter to M. de Sire is, indeed, a remarkable one; but it should be read in its entirety to be thoroughly appreciated.[2] In it Schumann speaks of the greater facility which came to him with repeated practice as a composer. But he concludes, with customary modesty, by begging his correspondent not to place him between Beethoven and Weber, "but somewhere near them," so that he might still continue, throughout his life, to learn more from them.

[1] *See* page 191.
[2] See *The Life of Schumann told in His Letters*.

CHAPTER IV

Aspiration to a Title—The Newly-Fledged " Doctor "—Wieck's Persistent Opposition—A Wedding Day at last—A Piano Presentation—Song, Symphony and Chamber Music—Longing for an Opera Text—Composition of " Paradise and the Peri "—Mendelssohn and the " Peri "—" Paradise and the Peri " a Unique Work.

Aspiration to a Title

DURING all this period the opposition of Friedrich Wieck to his daughter Clara's marriage with Schumann continued. Not even the fact that the musician was rising to eminence as critic and composer could incline the heart of the obdurate father towards him. It was, perhaps, natural that the old man, owing to his pardonable pride in a gifted daughter who was fast winning quite a European reputation as an executant, should be unwilling to consent to the possible termination of her brilliant public career if she united herself to a man who, although unquestionably talented, held, as yet, no position or title of distinction. Schumann seems to have realised this. Early in 1838 he conceived the idea of getting a Doctor's degree conferred upon him by the University of Leipzig. The motives of the composer, in aspiring to this dignity, appear to have been actuated solely by his love for, and pride in, his *fiancée*, and not by personal vanity—if we judge the point through the lines contained within a letter[1] to his sister-in-law, Thérèse Schumann, in which, having referred to Clara Wieck's decoration as Court Pianist,[2] he says that although personally he would desire nothing beyond what his art had made him, yet, for the sake of the pleasure that it would give the parents on both sides, he would like to have some titular distinction. A year afterwards[3] we find him inquiring definitely from Keferstein upon what conditions and terms the University would grant him a Doctor's degree. In particular he expresses a hope that the honour may be conferred upon him in recognition of some work already accomplished either as essayist, or musician, or both; and especially he seems anxious that, if possible, the title might take the form of *Doctor of Music.* He also asks Keferstein to put in a good word with the authorities on his behalf, and he seems to have sent his friend some of his writings and certain honorary diplomas as a guarantee of personal ability and worth.[4]

The Newly-Fledged "Doctor"

To hear genius thus pleading for recognition is touching; but it is an oft-repeated story. Still oftener, if there be not friends and influence behind, do we find that such appeals are made in vain, and nothing is then left to the creative mind but to carve out its own way to appreciation, unaided and alone. Schumann was, however, more fortunate. After a trifling delay he was made Doctor of Philosophy *honoris causa*—a tribute to his general culture which seems to have

[1] March 25, 1838.
[2] To the Emperor of Austria.
[3] About February 1840.
[4] He had been elected member of certain musical societies in Leipzig and Stuttgart.

delighted the recipient very much. In a letter of thanks to Keferstein he expresses himself pleased, and speaks of having at once sent the news to his betrothed, who at the time was on tour, and whom he describes as being just such a child as to dance with delight at the idea of being engaged to marry a Doctor! We smile also at the writer's own boyish glee in signing himself in this letter, and some that follow, as "Dr" Robert Schumann. It seems a pity that his request, that the title should take the form of a *musical* one, could not have been granted, probably owing to the fact that Continental universities do not appear to recognise music as a faculty, as British universities now agree in doing. When pleading that he might be decorated in reference to his beloved calling, Schumann had mentioned to Keferstein that, during the two preceding years, he had written some 400 pages of music which was, for the most part, published—surely a sufficient guarantee of his creative musicianship!

Wieck's Persistent Opposition

Yet even the high University distinction, won by acknowledged and richly-deserving merit and achievement in polite learning generally, could not move Wieck. The trials of the lovers were, indeed, severe. Some time previously, owing to the persistent refusal of Clara's father to permit the wedding of the faithful couple to take place, Schumann, with extreme reluctance, had been obliged to appeal to the Court for sanction to marry apart from the consent of his *fiancée's* father. How much such a proceeding must have pained the sensitive natures of both gifted artists may well be imagined. That Schumann's highly nervous and emotional temperament was much perturbed is keenly evident from many letters written to friends and relatives at this period. To Dorn he speaks of the whole affair being "a wretched story" in that because he (Schumann) was not a Von Rothschild, Wieck continued to forbid the banns. For months it appears that the painful case dragged on, during which time, as editor and musician, Schumann was making most strenuous efforts to effect worthy provision for his future home, which ever, like the *ignis fatuus*, seemed further off as attempts were made to reach it.

Wedding Day at Last

At length, after many delays and suspense, Schumann having satisfactorily proved that his income was sufficient to support a wife, the decision of the Court was given in the favour of the suppliants; and at last, on September 12, 1840, Robert Schumann and Clara Wieck were made man and wife. The date upon which the happy event took place was considered, with his usual belief in "lucky days," as a propitious one by the composer, as it was the eve of his betrothed's twenty-first birthday. On that day he had desired that she should be his own; and thus, after long waiting and many trials, did the happy event befall. So impressed was the joyous bridegroom with the month number of his bride's natal day that, writing on his wedding day, the 12th, to an old friend, Robert Friese, he dates the letter (in advance) the 13th of September 1840! In the short note referred to Schumann begs Friese to think kindly of him and his Clara between the hours of ten and eleven, and to wish them every blessing.

Robert and Clara Schumann.

A pleasing little incident that took place some short time before the marriage is of interest as showing at once the thoughtfulness and the devotion of Schumann. From musician to musician, especially when the receiver was so brilliant and accomplished a pianist as Clara Wieck, no gift from her lover could be imagined more appropriate than a pianoforte. This Schumann purchased for her —a Härtel Grand—but his mode of presenting it was the most charming part of all. He arranged the arrival of the instrument as a surprise to the recipient. The way in which matters were managed is best learnt from an interesting letter[1] of the composer's to the firm of Messrs Breitkopf & Härtel, from whom the piano had been purchased. In this epistle he mentions that at half-past four upon an appointed day he will call to take his betrothed for a walk. Between that hour and six he requests that the instrument should be delivered at Clara's residence. The delight of the girl may be imagined when she returned with her lover to find such a suitable present awaiting her acceptance. We can well believe that some delightful music followed, and that the appropriate gift, as well as the graceful way in which it was given, was highly appreciated.

Piano Presentation

That the marriage of the two young musicians was a supremely happy one none can doubt. A more ideal union could scarcely be imagined than that of a creative and an executive artist, both of the first rank, whose aims were of the highest and whose artistic sympathies tended to the advancement of pianoforte music in its noblest

[1] July 4, 1840.

and most poetic aspects. We are not surprised then to find that the opening years of Schumann's married life mark the most active, as the most varied, period of his musical output and editorial labours. In 1840, his marriage year, having previously confined his attention almost exclusively to pianoforte music, the composer bursts into ecstatic song. Over a hundred *Lieder* are traced to this period, all of them charming, and, in the opinion of many, representing Schumann, as melodist and harmonist, in his happiest and most spontaneous vein.

Song, Symphony and Chamber Music

In 1841, Symphony form seems to have particularly attracted him. During this year he wrote no less than three; and an important event was the performance of his B flat Symphony at a concert given by his wife at the Gewandhaus, Leipzig, with Mendelssohn conducting. 1842 saw him active in yet another department of creative output — Chamber Music. The rapidity with which he wrote at this time was marvellous. Three string Quartets were completed within a month. These were dedicated to Mendelssohn. Ferdinand David, the famous violinist and friend of Mendelssohn, seems to have been frankly and sincerely delighted with them. There is no doubt but that this appreciation pleased the composer, though he received the praise lavished upon him in his characteristic modest spirit.

It was in this year also that the beautiful Quintet for pianoforte and strings (Op. 44) saw the light. Among some famous contemporaries who heard this work, and who appeared to have been favourably impressed by it, was the great French composer, Berlioz, who was in Leipzig when it was first performed, with Madame Schumann at the piano, early in the year of 1843. As Berlioz was known to have been scathing in his remarks about the music of Mendelssohn and other German artists, his favourable opinion of Schumann is worthy of note. Eccentric and defiant as the gifted Frenchman was, he was undoubtedly original. He favoured daring tone-painting and so-called "programme" music of a poetic and fanciful kind. In all these respects, if from a differing artistic standpoint as might be expected from his strong and somewhat fiery temperament, Berlioz resembled Schumann. It is also to be noted that both were musical journalists of considerable acumen and brilliancy. Among other Schumann compositions of this year were the well-known Pianoforte Quartet (Op. 47), and a Pianoforte Trio.

Longing for an Opera Text

The year 1843, to which so much chamber music belonged, seems indeed to have been a very prolific and generally busy one. Not only was editorial work pressing, but new forms of composition were powerfully occupying the musician's mind. Hitherto, with the exception of the burst of jubilant song which marked his marriage year, Schumann had restricted himself to instrumental music. It will have been observed how first the pianoforte, next the orchestra, and lastly the string quartet suggested sound pictures to the tone-painter. In the early spring of 1843 it seems certain that the construction of great choral works was in his mind. For some considerable time he had been contemplating an opera. The trouble was, as it always has been with the great Masters, to get a suitable libretto. On the 31st October 1841, Schumann, in writing to Dr Robert Griepenkerl,[1] had begged him for an opera text, telling his correspondent, in his impetuous way, how much he longed for a good book. But if he was not destined to get his heart's desire immediately in regard to a work for the stage, the idea of a great composition of somewhat similar *genre* was suggested to him in reading Thomas Moore's *Lalla Rookh.* Therein he found the charming phantasy of "Paradise and the Peri"; and the even flow of the musical verse, as also the vivid and spiritual imagery of the Irish poet, at once appealed to the emotional imagination of Schumann. The result was that, having himself arranged and adapted the text to suit his purpose, he conceived the plan of writing an oratorio on the subject. He speaks in a letter to Kossmaly of being at this time busy over a great work, describing it as, indeed, one of the most important he had hitherto attempted. Detailing the nature of the task he writes that it is *not* an opera, but rather "a new departure for the concert-room."[2] Later on, the term "profane oratorio" was the title given to "Paradise and the Peri."

This work inspired the composer very much and was

[1] Author of the musical novel, *Das Musikfest, oder die Beethovener*, which Schumann calls a "lovable creation," only objecting to the dedication to Meyerbeer, towards whom he cherished an artistic aversion.

[2] Letter, May 5, 1843.

written rapidly. Commenced in the spring of 1843, at the beginning of June we find him informing Dr E. Krüger that so busy had he been writing notes (*i.e.*, musical notes) that he was in danger of forgetting how to form letters! In this interesting epistle[1] he gives Ascension Day of the year as the time about which he had finished his *magnum opus*, and he describes it particularly as "an oratorio; not for the conventicle, but for bright, happy people." The writing of the work seems to have considerably enthralled him, for he adds that, while composing it, he was aware of a voice which seemed to whisper to him, "It is not quite in vain, what you are doing!" Probably a little polishing and re-writing was done subsequently, for about a fortnight later[2] we find him telling his friend Verhulst that, a few days previously, he had finished "Paradise and the Peri," having written *Fine* at the end of the score with deep thankfulness to Heaven that his energies had been so well maintained throughout. Once more he mentions his impression that this work was one of the best and greatest he had hitherto penned; and he comments upon the immense amount of labour entailed in putting together a score of such dimensions, adding that, only after completing it, did he realise what a feat Mozart must have accomplished in writing eight operas within so short a period of time.

Composition of "Paradise and the Peri"

"Paradise and the Peri" was first performed, under the composer's own direction, on December 4, 1843. So great seems to have been the success of this, its first public

[1] Letter, June 3, 1843. [2] Letter, June 19, 1843.

rendering, that a repetition performance was given a week later (December 11th). It was for this occasion that Madame Schumann wrote to Mendelssohn, inviting him to be present. Her letter, however, seems not to have reached Schumann's famous contemporary in time. Mendelssohn appears, from his reply, to have been genuinely sorry not to have been a listener on this occasion. "I am quite too disappointed about it" (*i.e.*, at getting the letter of invitation too late), he writes. Then he begs Madame Schumann to tell her husband how heartily he rejoiced to hear of the splendid success of the new work. "Every one who wrote to me," he continues, "was full of the 'Peri' and the pleasure it had given," and he adds that the lady is to tell Schumann that he (Mendelssohn) looked upon this triumph as good fortune that had befallen himself. While Mendelssohn's sincerity must be believed in thus expressing himself, it is to be regretted that circumstances prevented him from honouring the occasion with his presence and so paying a graceful tribute to a fellow-composer who was one of his own warmest and most appreciative admirers.

Mendelssohn and the "Peri"

On the 23rd of the same month (December) "Paradise and the Peri" was again heard, this time at the Dresden Opera House. It is clear that Schumann was at this time a well-known and respected personage in the musical circles of his native land. The work itself was a notable one. That its composition had interested and fascinated him very much seems evident from correspondence of his own on the subject. It is indeed certain that his

"Paradise & the Peri" a Unique Work

poetic fancy was much attracted by Moore's poem, which he speaks of as "one of the sweetest flowers of English verse." The unique character of the work is also to be remembered. The term "profane oratorio" has been applied to it, though some might prefer to describe it as a sacred cantata, or else a *secular* oratorio. But no one of these terms, perhaps, are quite appropriate in this case to the minds of those who know the work well. Schumann's own description of "a new departure for the concert room"[1] is that most adapted to classify a composition at once lyrical, emotional and more ethereal than possessing the sacred-writ dignity of Oratorio or the dramatic and mundane elements of Cantata.

[1] *See* page 50.

CHAPTER V

The Climax of Exertion—Letter from Russia to "Papa Wieck"—A Trip to England contemplated—Professorship at Leipzig Conservatoire—A Move to Dresden—Contrapuntal Work—Looking for a Libretto—The Writing of "Genoveva"—The Composer and His Opera—Delays and Postponements—"Genoveva" performed at last—The "Faust" Music—Conducting Choral Societies.

The Climax of Exertion

HERE we reach a period of Schumann's life when the great strain of creative exertion in two departments—that of editor and composer—was beginning, perhaps, to tell upon a sensitive and highly-strung nature which, in its ceaseless mental output, was doubtless over-straining energies more mercurial than robust. Not that Schumann had suffered much of the "wear and tear" of the artist's life. Want of adequate means was never a serious trouble to him, as was the case with more than one of his compeers, nor was he much before the public in a social or personal sense. The first four years of his married life were spent almost in complete retirement—his literary and musical labours fully occupying his attention. Outside the home circle and its environments he took but little interest in mundane matters. Nor did he ever, at this or any other time, attempt to shine as a conversationalist or figure in society. To a few familiar friends Schumann could unburden himself; but he did so with more ease in correspondence than in speech. It was with difficulty that his wife could persuade him to accompany her on some of her brilliantly successful concert tours. Yet the need at this time that he should have rest and change of scene made her urge him all the more, when a Russian journey was anticipated in 1844, to go with her; and this he somewhat reluctantly consented to do. Once started, however, he got out of himself and thoroughly enjoyed the trip.

Letter from Russia to "Papa Wieck"

This tour to the land of the Czar—upon which Schumann and his gifted wife started on January 26, 1844—was an eminently successful one. Madame Schumann appeared in several towns, including St Petersburg and Moscow, and was highly appreciated and enthusiastically received everywhere. Some time before, a complete reconciliation had taken place between Wieck and his daughter Clara; and although Schumann felt it difficult to resume the old friendly familiarity which a near relationship still further intensified, it is evident that, previous to 1844, the past had been happily condoned on both sides. Doubtless the arrival of two little grandchildren—daughters who had been born to the Schumanns—turned the hearts of the elder and the younger man to each other. Anyway it is evident that, from letters written to "Papa Wieck" on the Russian journey, father-in-law and son-in-law were once more on a becoming footing with each other. In these communications we get much interesting information about the gratifying reception which Schumann and his wife received wherever they went, especially at St Petersburg, where Clara had given four concerts and played before the Empress. Schumann affords his father-in-law a most interesting glimpse of the artistic standing of the Russian capital, where all depended upon the favour of the Court and the *haute volée*, and the Press could do but little. At the time of the Schumanns' visit to St Petersburg it appears that Italian Opera was the rage, and that Madame Garcia was the prime favourite. Thus it had happened that Madame Schumann's first two concerts had not been so well attended; but the third, and especially the fourth—which was given at the Michael Theatre and seems to have attracted the notice of several aristocratic amateurs—left nothing to be desired in the way of enthusiastic patronage. Schumann, in one of his letters, mentions especially the kindness which they had received from the distinguished brothers Wielhorsky, both of whom were on daily intimacy at the Imperial Court. The Prince of Oldenburg (nephew of the Emperor) and his wife are then referred to as having warmly patronised the two famous artists. "They" (the Oldenburgs), writes Schumann,[1] "showed us over their palace themselves yesterday." The two Counts Wielhorsky also organised a *soirée* with orchestra in honour of the Schumanns, and at this the composer's Symphony was performed. It seems that the Pianoforte Quartet (Op. 47) was dedicated to Count Mathieu Wielhorsky, whom, with his brother Michael, Schumann describes as very excellent and genial amateurs. Probably the Henselts, who were

[1] Letter, April 1, 1844.

then resident in St Petersburg and familiar with Prince Oldenburg, and whom Schumann speaks of as being particularly friendly, did much in the way of introducing the two gifted artists to these high-placed patrons. Other little incidents of the Russian tour which Schumann details in his home letter were the popularity of Mendelssohn's "Frühlingslied" (Spring Song), which Madame Schumann was asked to repeat everywhere; the meeting with Schumann's maternal uncle, Schnabel; the expenses of living at St Petersburg; and their anticipated fears of a journey to Moscow—which afterwards passed off pleasurably enough. Altogether the letter referred to was a bright, delightful and informative one, such as Schumann could pen so well when in good health and humour.

Trip to England contemplated

For a while, indeed, after his return from Russia, Schumann was much benefited by the change, and wrote in good spirits to his many friends. He even contemplated an early trip to England on his own account. He was desirous of bringing out "Paradise and the Peri" in London, as it had, as he says himself, "sprung from English soil." There had been some correspondence with Moscheles[1] on the subject, and Mendelssohn encouraged Schumann in the project. Nothing came of it, however, owing to difficulties in producing the work with English words. Schumann was keenly disappointed, as he had a strong hankering to visit London. This desire was never gratified.

[1] January 27, 1844.

One piece of news that gave him pleasure was that Queen Victoria liked his music and had his B flat Symphony played by the Windsor private band. He subsequently thought of dedicating his "Manfred" music to her, but this was not carried through.

Upon the opening of the Leipzig Conservatoire on April 3, 1843, Schumann was appointed a professor of composition. Little is known of him as a teacher.[1] Carl Ritter, a former pupil of Hiller, was under him for a time, and Schumann wrote to Hiller to say that the young student had made some progress with him. Beyond this personal testimony we look in vain for information respecting Schumann as a teacher. It is probable that, like most creative minds, he found the art of instruction ill suited to his temperament and inclination. It is one thing to know how to do a thing by instinct—and it is thus that genius knows—but it is quite another matter to impart such knowledge to the ordinary learner. Schumann felt this, as many expressions in his letters and essays clearly show, and doubtless he was conscientiously relieved when (failing health necessitating his leaving Leipzig for a time) he decided to resign his professorship at the Conservatoire.

Professorship at Leipzig Conservatoire

A nervous ailment, which was kept in temporary abeyance by the trip to Russia, began to reassert itself with serious symptoms soon after Schumann's return home in the summer of 1844. His memory at times deserted him, and composing fatigued him greatly. At length he was obliged to give up work of all kind, including his

[1] We are not forgetting his *Hints to Young Musicians*—A. P.

editorial duties in connection with the *Neue Zeitschrift.* A move to Dresden was tried later in the year in order to recruit his shattered energies. Here the composer was less likely to live in an atmosphere of music, as was the case in Leipzig. Some friends, who saw him at this period, were distressed to notice how broken down in health he appeared to be. Sea bathing was tried, but only slowly did health and strength return. While in Dresden he saw a good deal of his friend, Ferdinand Hiller; and among interesting people whose acquaintance he made were Weber's widow and Wagner. About this time "Tannhäuser" was produced, and Schumann, although he speaks highly of the work, deplored Wagner's lack of melody therein! Likely, owing to their vast difference of temperament, the two composers never cultivated any great measure of personal intimacy.[1] Schumann, it is to be remembered, was generally reserved as a conversationalist, and he was, perhaps, at this time, not being in good health, less communicative than ever.

Move to Dresden

As soon, however, as he was pronounced convalescent, once more the active brain of the musician turned to creative work, and, as if to make up for lost time, Schumann occupied himself with the severer contrapuntal forms, writing, before the year 1846, his Studies and Sketches for Pedal Pianoforte (Op. 56 and Op. 58), six Fugues on the name of Bach (Op. 60), and the four Pianoforte Fugues (Op. 72). To this period also belongs the C major Symphony (Op. 61) produced by Mendelssohn at the Gewandhaus

Contrapuntal Work

[1] *See* pages 132 and 144.

Concerts, Leipzig, on November 5, 1846. After so much purely imaginative writing in his earlier works, that Schumann should have reverted to strict forms at this time is striking and suggestive. Doubtless, in the more mechanical structure of the fugue, he found not only wholesome exercise for contemplation and memory, but also a respite from that striving for vivid imagery which often too powerfully affected his emotional nature. The musical paper no longer occupied him, since he retired from the editorship of the *Neue Zeitschrift* in 1844.

Looking for a Libretto

The success of the "Peri," which greatly gratified the composer, suggested to him, upon his complete recovery, the undertaking of a work suitable for the stage. Even previous to the Russian tour he had been in consultation with his friend Zuccalmaglio over likely plots, and as early as 1841 [1] he had asked Dr Griepenkerl for an opera text. In the September of 1842 he wrote that German opera was the subject of his "morning and evening prayer." In the New Year of 1844 we gather, from a letter of the composer to Zuccalmaglio,[2] that the latter had suggested "Mokanna" (another "Moore" subject) and "The Invasion of Spain by the Moors." The latter seems to have appealed most of all to Schumann, and he wrote to his friend to the effect that he would be very pleased to find the book ready for him upon his return from Russia in May of that year. Nothing, however, appears to have come of the correspondence. Commencing with the year 1847, and for some years afterwards, Schumann compiled a "Theaterbüchlein," in which he

[1] *See* page 50. [2] Letter, January 22, 1844.

jotted down his impressions of certain operas heard during that period. At length, upon reading the tragedies of Tiecke and Hebbel on that subject, he was much struck with the legend of St Geneviève. He endeavoured to get Robert Reinick, the poet, to draw up a suitable book of words from Hebbel's version, but the result was far from satisfactory. He then approached Hebbel himself on the matter, and tried to persuade him to revise or recast Reinick's work. Hebbel, though strongly attracted to Schumann himself, somewhat resented the cutting down of his work to suit lyric requirements. Finally Schumann, like Berlioz and Wagner, had to turn his own librettist, and thus he wrote his own "book" of "Genoveva."

That he was yet far from well is evident; and probably "Genoveva" did not progress so rapidly in its evolution as did his earlier "profane oratorio," "Paradise and the Peri." In a letter [1] to Verhulst he speaks of having been very busy from January to August of 1848 over his opera "Genoveva," feeling, when he had finished it, that he had, on the whole, been successful in the expression of his musical ideas therein.

The Opera "Genoveva"

The same epistle speaks of occasional fits of melancholy, which music, however, is effectual in driving away; and he also mentions the many blessings of his home circle—his good wife, beloved little ones—a son had lately been born to him—and the general musical activity of his life. Further, in regard to the newly-completed opera, he expresses his strong desire to see and hear it, adding that, as yet, he had

[1] Letter, November 4, 1848.

taken no definite steps about getting it produced, on account of the then "stormy" aspect of the world. Other works of this busy year had been the "Album for the Young," the composition of which had given him pleasure, and which he hoped would prove to be a most successful publication.

The ultimate production of "Genoveva" was, however, destined to cause him worry and annoyance. He decided to have it brought out at Leipzig, where he felt the people were kindly disposed towards him, and with that view he put himself in communication with Conductor Julius Rietz. Some correspondence having passed, and a promise being given that the opera should be mounted, Schumann appears to have been slightly apprehensive that the matter was not being taken up by the directors with sufficient enthusiasm. So, on the 21st November, he wrote to Rietz to beg him to fulfil his promise (*i.e.*, of performing the work) as soon as possible. With that spirit of modesty which is only found with the highest genius, he declared himself willing to sacrifice anything in the music that might interfere with the dramatic action, his great desire being that Rietz—who perhaps had shown him some coldness or formality about the matter—would take the project up with sufficient warmth to ensure a rendition early in the ensuing year. The fact that a form of agreement, drawn up by Schumann, is appended to this communication, points to the musician's legal studies as conducive to business-like habits. In this agreement he stipulates (*a*) for the performance of the work upon an early date to be mutually agreed upon; (*b*) that the proceeds from the sale of the libretto, which he purposed to have printed at his own expense, should remain the composer's property; and (*c*) that the fee for performing rights was to be paid to the composer on the day of the performance.[1]

Delays and Postponements

This agreement was not carried out. In the sketch referred to Schumann had named February 15, 1849, as a probable date for the production of the work. But February arrived, and there was a postponement of the promised performance. Schumann speaks[2] of being very much annoyed about this; and later on there was no satisfactory information from either Rietz or the manager of the theatre with regard to the date of the production of his work. The entire matter troubled him considerably. He complains bitterly to his friend Härtel that the whole winter had been wasted over the procrastination of the appearance of his opera, and thus he had been unable to bring out any of his latest works at Leipzig, where he was always sure of a gratifying reception. Easter of the year passed, and yet there was no word of his opera being staged. In a letter to Brendel he confesses to having heard that the delay was caused by *the intrigues of local musicians.* But, like the honest, unsuspecting and thoroughly generous soul that he was, he disbelieved this, and pleaded the honesty and straightforwardness of his own motives in art.[3] Later on, apparently, some mischief-maker wrote to Schumann with regard to Rietz, but the composer refuted the gossip by writing directly to the Leipzig conductor, telling him of the

[1] In full in letter to Rietz, November 21, 1848.
[2] Letter to Dr Härtel, February 7, 1849.
[3] *See* the entire letter referred to in *The Life of Robert Sehumann told in His Letters.*

tale-bearing that was going on, and assuring him that, when the ill-disposed missive arrived, he (Schumann) had said to his wife, "That is a lie." Even had there been any truth in the report, doubtless the friendly candour of Schumann —in refusing to harbour an unworthy suspicion of one concerning whom, as an artist, he expressed admiration, and, as a man, in whom he reposed faith—spurred Rietz on to a tardy fulfilment of his promise. Anyway, definite arrangements seem to have been made forthwith for the mounting of the long-delayed opera in the summer of the year. But fate seemed to be against its production. At the time arranged Schumann found himself unable to attend owing to a domestic circumstance.

"Genoveva" performed (1850)

So time dragged on, Schumann protesting and the management putting him off with evasive promises. At last, keenly exasperated by the continued postponements, the composer, in a communication to Dr Härtel in the beginning of 1850, said he felt inclined to compel the theatre folk to keep faith with him, if only by threatening to make public the circumstances of the case. But friends, happily, dissuaded him from taking such a course and also from going to law about it. Finally, "Genoveva" was produced, under Schumann's own direction, at the Leipzig Theatre on June 25, 1850. The time was unfavourable. It was the summer season, and, as the composer said, people preferred to be in the woods. There was, nevertheless, a large attendance; but the reception of the work, although complimentary to a musician who was highly respected at Leipzig, could scarcely be called enthusiastic.

Spohr alone, who had attended many of the rehearsals, was thoroughly appreciative. Certainly the fact that Schumann had, in "Genoveva," done away with the conventional operatic recitative, appealed to the famous violinist-composer, who approved of the innovation and had adopted it himself. But one eminent musician's decision could not sway the balance of public opinion. There were, in all, only three representations of the opera; and the whole affair seems to have left Schumann much distressed and annoyed. Dr E. Krüger wrote an unfavourable *critique* of the work in the *Neue Zeitschrift.* The opinions therein expressed so vexed Schumann that he penned, for him, an exceedingly sharp letter to the critic, the consequence of which was that the friendship between the two terminated. It is to be remembered that Schumann was particularly sensitive to adverse criticism, and also that his health and nerves, far from robust at the time, had been severely tried by the worries and annoyances which the production of his opera cost him.

"Faust" Music

Another important work, belonging to this period, gave Schumann more satisfaction. He was powerfully attracted, as so many other composers have been, by Goethe's immortal "Faust" poem. The end of the second part, the Salvation of Faust, especially fascinated him. He commenced to write the "Faust" music in 1844—a time when he may be said to have entered upon his maturity as a composer. The composition of the whole extended over some nine years —the mystic *nine* again!—different parts being composed in 1849, 1850 and as late as 1853. The earlier portion was performed privately in Dresden on June 25, 1848. Writing to Nottebohm [1] of this event, he speaks of the pleasure which the rendering of the work gave him, and mentions that he considered the music to have made an even greater impression than that of the "Peri," probably on account of the grandeur of Goethe's noble language. He expressed himself similarly to his friend Brendel,[2] adding that what gratified him most was to hear so many of the audience say that the musical setting had first made the poem clear to them. A year later, on the hundredth anniversary of Goethe's birthday, August 28, 1849, "Faust" was heard, with added scenes, at a Festival Concert in Dresden (Mendelssohn's "First Walpurgis Night" being also included in the programme), at Leipzig on the 29th, and similarly at Weimar—both in celebration of the same event. Schumann's music seems to have been much liked at Dresden; but it was heard with varying opinions at Leipzig and Weimar. The composer, always eager for appreciation in the town of the Gewandhaus Concerts, was disappointed that Leipzig did not receive the work so favourably as he had hoped. He writes [3] to tell Brendel that nothing could have been more satisfactory than its performance and reception at Dresden. In this letter he mentions that the chorus-singing had been excellent. The solo singers named were Fräulein Schwarzbach and Herr Weixelstorfer — Mutterwurzer the composer particularly commends for his singing of the air (with harp accompaniment) allotted to Dr Marinus. "The audience," says

[1] Letter, July 3, 1848.
[2] Letter of same date.
[3] September 1, 1849.

Schumann, "listened with rapt attention." Speaking of the several "Faust" performances to Dr Härtel, the composer declared that he would have liked to have had Faust's cloak for the day, so as to have heard it everywhere. He stated also, as a curious fact, that the work had been laid away in his desk for five years, and had been almost forgotten by him, when it found at last a suitable occasion for performance at this great celebration. The Overture to "Faust" was not written until 1853, when the whole work, with added scenes, was finally divided into three parts. It was not published until 1858, when the composer was, alas! no more. The first performance of the work in its entirety took place in December 1862 at the Gewandhaus Concerts, under the *bâton* of Carl Reineke.

Conducting Choral Societies

Besides composition, another element of musical activity had come into the composer's life, during his residence in Dresden, which is worthy of note. Shortly after "Genoveva" began to occupy him, Schumann had undertaken the conducting of local choral societies. His friend Hiller, upon leaving Dresden to fulfil an appointment at Düsseldorf, transferred the duties of conducting a Dresden male voice choir to Schumann. For a time the composer enjoyed the work entailed. In any case it suggested his writing three Songs of War and Liberty (Op. 62) and seven Vocal Canons to words by Rückert (Op. 65). There is also to be noted, in this connection, a Motet for double chorus of male voices (Op. 93). But the drilling of the male choir was work that could not long appeal to him. As he says, he scarcely felt in his element at the rehearsals. He speaks[1] of not caring to hear those perpetual chords of $^{6}_{4}$, necessitated by male part-song writing, after a long day of music-making. A "mixed" chorus, which he afterwards got together himself, afforded him a much more congenial field of action. His "Faust" music, as his "Paradise and the Peri," were performed by this body of picked singers, who numbered from sixty to seventy voices. Duties of this description took the composer "out of his shell" more than formerly, and he was even persuaded at times to join in social festivities with his chorus-singers. On one occasion he writes to his friend Ferdinand David in pleasant anticipation of a picnic which he and his wife were organising in connection with the choir.

[1] Letter to Verhulst, November 4, 1848.

CHAPTER VI

Retrospective—The Composer as Conductor—The Apathy of Vienna—The Shadow of the End—From Dresden to Düsseldorf—A Pleasant Start in the New Sphere—Congenial Occupation—As Conductor—Failing Health—Compositions of the Time.

BEFORE speaking of the events which followed 1850, the last year of his residence in Dresden, a brief retrospective glance at Schumann's career may not here be out of place. From his earliest childhood music was struggling within him for pre-eminence. The literary pursuits, and especially the poetic tendencies, of his youth—aroused by the romantic sentimentality of such imaginative writers as Jean Paul—invested his mind with a wealth of emotional thought and intense striving for a lofty idealism which, even in his young manhood, tended to keep him as a being apart from intimate social converse with his fellow men. Strong counteracting forces that opposed this self-seclusion were to be found in his editorial labours; the keen sympathy of his refined nature, which instinctively attracted many kindred spirits within his almost forbidden circle of confidence; and, notably, his great love for Clara Wieck, under whose beneficent influence he undoubtedly

Retrospective

poured forth the noblest achievement of his genius. But his keen sensitiveness sustained many shocks in his intercourse with the world—even from those within his own immediate circle. His mother's strong opposition to his following a chosen career, the utter uncongeniality of his University (legal) studies, the long waiting and struggle for his wife, the inevitable worries and anxieties connected with his editing of the *Neue Zeitschrift*, his vain effort to make a home for it and himself in Vienna—these and other petty worries were so many indentations upon an impressionable surface which even comparatively easy circumstances and the ultimate fulfilment of his most ardent desires could not efface. Dr Spitta [1] speaks of Schumann as being predisposed to worry. Such natures find it difficult to recruit, especially if they are somewhat morbidly inclined to hug the luxury of grief. Even when the greatest good falls into the lap, gloomy anticipations of possible mishaps will blight a life's happiness in its budding time. The most tranquil period of Schumann's life was probably that from 1840 to 1844. This commenced with his marriage, included his Song, Symphony and Chamber Music period, and culminated in the composition and successful performance of his one oratorio, "Paradise and the Peri." In 1844 came that trying breakdown of nerve and health which, for a time, suspended all active labours. His half-dozen years' residence in Dresden were, in many ways, a new phase of life for the composer. At first his physical and mental well-being demanded a pause of well-earned rest. But, once recruited, so incessant

[1] "Schumann" in *Dictionary of Music and Musicians* (Grove).

was the spurring on of the voice within for action, that new forms and new kinds of exertion evolved themselves out of surroundings. Thus pianoforte music in the stricter contrapuntal forms belongs to this time, and dramatic music—including "Genoveva," "Faust" and "Manfred"—were all written at this period. In the year 1849 Schumann's creative gifts reached their maximum of output. He was said in that year to have been able to write anywhere and anyhow. Some thirty works of all varieties—vocal, instrumental and orchestral—are to be catalogued within this twelvemonth, the prolific speed with which he executed some of them being remarkable. Even concentration and quietude were not now such needful adjuncts to him. In a letter to Dr Härtel, on the 23rd June 1849, he speaks of composing the song, "Kennst du das Land," in the midst of noisy children, though certainly not without inspiration.[1]

Schumann as Conductor

Before his Dresden sojourn, Schumann had only been before the public prominently as writer and composer. We then find him employed, as has already been stated, in the new capacity of choir-trainer and conductor. That he was genuinely interested in his chorus drilling, and especially in his mixed choral society, seems evident. We have spoken of this work as being a factor to draw him pleasurably, in a social way, from too close commune with his own thoughts. In a letter to Brendel in 1848, shortly after his Dresden choir had given the admirable private rendering of the "Faust" music already alluded to,[2] Schumann speaks of his societies being a great delight

[1] Quoted in the Published Letters.

[2] Page 66.

to him. He commends them for their ability in reading Beethoven's "Missa Solemnis" at first sight, talks of the pleasure it gives him to lead the singers "over hedges and ditches," and refers to their powers in studying new works, such as Gade's "Comala," which Schumann speaks of in the highest terms as deserving of a laurel wreath.

So much indeed did conducting interest him that, hearing a report that Rietz—who had been appointed after Mendelssohn's death to preside over the Gewandhaus Concerts—was about to accept Nicolai's place at Berlin, he (Schumann) at once made inquiries as to whether the directors would be likely to favour his application for the post if it were vacant. Nothing came of this, however, as Rietz decided to remain on at Leipzig. Immediately upon his recovery from the nervous prostration of the years 1844 and 1845, the musician seems, indeed, to have been more anxious than at any other time of his life for some regular routine of duties. Thus we find him applying for information to Nottebohm about the vacant Directorship at the Vienna Conservatoire in the July of 1847, mentioning that a post of the kind would be just the sort of a position he would like. But his destiny did not lie Viennawards.

Apathy of Vienna

The apathy of Vienna towards Schumann is difficult to understand, especially as he himself had always a strong affection for the art-loving Austrian capital. We have seen how, owing mainly to censorship, he was obliged to relinquish his hopes of establishing the *Neue Zeitschrift* there. In 1846 he and Madame Schumann had paid a professional visit to Vienna, and had been but indifferently received. Speaking of this to Brendel,[1] he mentions the performance of "Paradise and the Peri" as being sadly handicapped by the fact that, owing to the sudden refusal to sing of the two theatrical artists who had been engaged for the solo parts, these had to be given to amateurs who, according to the composer, "barely hit the notes, to say nothing of other things."[2]

How trying such an experience must have been to the sensitive ear of Schumann, one can well understand. It did indeed seem as if the chances were against Vienna learning to appreciate him as he deserved.

Shadow of the End

Worries of this kind, coupled to the procrastinations, annoyances and disappointments received in connection with "Genoveva," must assuredly have been exceedingly painful in Schumann's case. It is also to be remembered that he had but barely recovered from a serious nervous illness, probably consequent upon the strain and anxieties of the years leading up to his relinquishing of the editorship of the *Neue Zeitschrift*. He appeared to reach the zenith of his creative powers in the year 1849, which was perhaps the most prolific of all as far as varied styles of composition went. That date also represents—with brief periods of return to his former strength—the commencement of the last few years of his all too short life, when the vivid brain became over-wrought, and the grand powers were obscured by their own very intensity, which, piercing, perhaps, beyond that imaginative border across which mortal mind

[1] Letter, February 20, 1847. [2] *Ibid.*

dare hardly venture with safety, the result was a sad shattering of nerves and premature decay.

From Dresden to Düsseldorf

We return to the year 1849, about the November of which letters passed between Schumann and his friend Hiller[1] as to whether he (Schumann) would care to accept the post of musical conductor at Düsseldorf which Hiller was about to resign. At first Schumann, though attracted by the proposal, seems to have been loath to break up his household at Dresden, and he asks for time before giving a decisive answer. Reports, too, reached him that the state of musical proficiency in Düsseldorf was at a low standard. This, however, was not so, as he discovered afterwards, for Hiller had accomplished excellent work there. Thus when, in the following year, 1850, Schumann moved with his family to the new sphere, he was surprised and delighted to find himself in command of a most intelligent and expert body of performers. In his preliminary correspondence with Hiller, a rather melancholy topic—one might almost call it a foreboding—is touched upon in one of the letters. He speaks of having looked up for some notice of Düsseldorf in an old geography and found that, among its buildings, there was the notice of three convents and a madhouse. He mentions having no objection to the former, but that the reading about the latter had made him feel quite distressed. Then he proceeds to explain why. It seemed that, a few

[1] Hiller had accepted the post of Chapel Master at Cologne, whither he went in 1850, having suggested and obtained the appointment of Schumann as his successor at Düsseldorf.

years previously, when the Schumanns were staying at Maxen, the composer found that his window commanded a view of the Sonnenstein.[1] He speaks of having thoroughly disliked the sight of it, and that its proximity quite spoilt the pleasure of his sojourn there. Then he mentions the necessity of his having to be very careful in guarding against melancholy impressions of that kind. He then draws the metaphor of the musician living on the "sunny heights" who can ill brook to look upon the darker aspects of life, especially if, as was the case with him, the imaginative faculty was a vivid one.[2]

Pleasant Start in the New Sphere

The first year or so, nevertheless, of the residence of Schumann and his family at Düsseldorf seemed to have given the lie to all gloomy prognostications and anticipation of indifferent musical successes. Arriving early in September of 1850, he and his wife were received with universal respect and esteem, and the entire surroundings seemed most congenial and appreciative. The opening concert of the season included portions from his "Genoveva" and "Paradise and the Peri," as well as some of his songs. On this occasion Julius Tausch conducted, and the event was, in every way, calculated to give the composer an honourable and gratifying introduction to his new round of duties. So pleased, indeed, were the directors at having secured his services, and so successful was this first season, that several extra concerts were arranged for, a notable feature of which, suggested by Schumann himself, was that at least one performance yearly should be devoted to the

[1] Lunatic Asylum. [2] Letter, December 3, 1849.

works of living composers. Thus was Schumann always true to the underlying principle of his own life—that disinterested generosity which was ever ready to give a helping hand to the young and unknown, and to encourage talent and genius, especially in days of struggle and misunderstanding. This had been his aim all along in the *Neue Zeitschrift*, and he had had more than one beneficent scheme in his head on behalf of composers in their dealings with publishers and theatrical *impressarii.*

Congenial Occupation

Thus the opening part of Schumann's Düsseldorf sojourn seems to have passed most pleasurably. In a letter[1] to Dr Klitzsch, he speaks of being very content in his present position, and mentions that, although he found conducting very fatiguing, what he had to do of it did not overtax his physical strength. Later in the same year,[2] when corresponding with Moscheles, who had dedicated his Sonata for Pianoforte and Violoncello (Op. 121) to the younger master, Schumann again refers to his surroundings as agreeable and suitable. In addition to his duties as orchestral conductor, he started a Chamber Music Society at Düsseldorf for the performance of important works both new and old. Thus there appeared to have been no diminution of his musical fervour and activity, and he tells Moscheles that he is happy at having found a field of action which suited him in so many respects.

Conducting was far from being Schumann's *forte.* Ere long this became evident, even to those who loved and admired him most. He was too sensitive and too poetical

[1] August 9, 1851. [2] November 20, 1851.

to bend his imagination to the mechanical part of beating time. It was also soon apparent that neither his health nor nerves could, for any continued length of time, stand the strain, physical and mental, which, more or less, falls upon one who wields the *bâton* with real success. Many of the necessary traits of the ideal conductor were wanting in his reserved and almost timid temperament. "He had," says Dr Philip Spitta,[1] "neither the collectedness and prompt presence of mind, nor the sympathetic faculty, nor the enterprising dash, without each of which *conducting* in the true sense is impossible. He even found a difficulty in starting at a given *tempo*; nay, he sometimes shrank from giving any initial beat, so that some energetic instrumentalist would begin without waiting for the signal without incurring Schumann's wrath." Schumann, we are further told, was incapable of going over difficult portions bit by bit and getting all perfect. He would repeat a whole movement again and again, if its first or reiterated rendition was not satisfactory, but he never trusted himself to make a long speech or to enter into details as to how such and such a passage should go. It was the old story of the inability of genius to give an explanation for its *raison d'être*. The thoughts of great creative minds are often too deep for words. Thus, as we have before noticed in the case of Schumann as instructor, the composer is seldom the best teacher. He knows, but cannot tell why or how much he knows. In particular was this the case with Schumann, whose keenly emotional, though

As Conductor

[1] "Schumann" in *Dictionary of Music and Musicians* (Grove).

reserved, mind shrank from intercourse with the outside world, and preferred to meditate upon and evolve his imaginings in musical and poetic thought rather than plead with other intelligences for a better understanding of his own.

Failing Health

Moreover, after the first two seasons or so of his residence in Düsseldorf, it is evident that Schumann was feeling far from well. The previous nervous breakdown, which had necessitated his migrating from Leipzig to Dresden for rest and change, threatened him at times again, and in a still graver form. A love for the occult and the mysterious — an outcome of his poetic and meditative nature—now led him into channels of thought and inquiry far from healthy for one of his intensely imaginative and somewhat superstitious nature. At this time he was deeply drawn to table-turning and spirit-rapping, and was much under the thraldom of dreams and omens. When writing to Hiller to arrange for the division of the conductor's duties at the Lower Rhine Festival of 1853, he was fuller of the results of his recent spiritualistic investigations than keen upon business detail. He mentions having tried *table-turning* for the first time shortly before, and being deeply interested in having received some remarkable message from the Unseen as to the rhythm and *tempo* of the C minor Symphony of Beethoven. The festival to which he referred was that held at Düsseldorf on the 15th, 16th and 17th of May 1853. On this occasion Schumann conducted the "Messiah" and his own D minor Symphony, Hiller wielding the *bâton* during the remaining performances. It was among the last of poor Schumann's successful public appearances. His illness seems to have been rapidly gaining ground. After a concert on October 27th, in the same year, an attempt was made to induce him to retire for a little while from the active exertion of conducting. But the hypersensitive musician misunderstood; and probably the brooding over an imaginary slight aggravated the ailments of those delicate imaginative and physical organisms which, in his case, were ill fitted to combat opposition or misapprehension of any kind.

Compositions of the Time

The Düsseldorf period was not, however, without its results in creative work. It saw the completion of the great E flat Symphony (Op. 97) popularly known as the "Rhenish." This noble tone picture was supposed to represent the composer's impression of a Festival at Cologne. It was given, for the first time, at Düsseldorf on the 6th of February 1851, and later on in the month at Cologne. But on neither occasion did it meet with a due meed of appreciation. It was not heard in England until the 4th December 1865, when the charms of its intense colouring and imagery were warmly admired at a concert given by Signor Arditi. That Schumann's works were gradually gaining ground and fascinating an ever-widening circle was evident. From March 14th to 21st of the year 1852 a "Schumann week" was given at Leipzig, and this, if it did not invoke universal enthusiasm, strongly attracted the highest artistic circles of the day, both Liszt and Joachim being keenly attentive listeners and admirers upon this occasion. In the year 1853 Schumann was much "heartened up" by a successful professional tour which he and his wife took through Holland. Writing to Joachim from Utrecht, on the 11th December 1853, Schumann speaks of having been most successful on this trip, having received a warm and gratifying welcome everywhere. "The Dutch public," he remarks, "is most enthusiastic, and their taste is, on the whole, of a high standard."[1]

[1] Letter, December 11, 1853.

CHAPTER VII

Sacred Music—The Composer's Scheme for "Luther"—Librettist and Musician—Further Compositions of the Time—Meeting with Brahms—A Last Yearning Viennawards—In the Valley of the Shadow—Release at Last—"The End is not yet."

WHILE in Düsseldorf Schumann was strongly drawn to compose sacred music. In 1849 he had written to Dr Krüger that he was turning his thoughts to the Church, but not without some diffidence. He had already set Rückert's Advent Hymn. The inhabitants of Düsseldorf were principally Catholic, and this probably induced Schumann to try his hand at a Mass (Op. 147) and a Requiem (Op. 148), both completed in 1852. He even hoped to do something on a still more ambitious scale. This was no less than a great oratorio, which was to be something rather out of the beaten track and a work that would attract all classes of people. The idea of this oratorio first came to him through his correspondence with Richard Pohl, an enthusiastic and gifted student of Natural History at the Leipzig University. Pohl had suggested "The Bride of Messina" as a possible text. Although Schumann could not see his way to an

Sacred Music

entire work on that subject, the idea inspired him towards activity in another direction. When writing to his young correspondent, he remarks that he would much like to compose an oratorio, and wonders if Pohl could assist him with a theme and book of words. "Luther," "Ziska," and a biblical theme are all suggested by the composer himself, and he adds quaintly that afterwards he might try a bright and amusing opera. The "Luther" idea was subsequently a good deal discussed, and appealed very forcibly to Schumann. In a letter of February 14, 1851, he speaks of it as "a tremendous subject," and one from which it would be necessary to abstract all ultramundane topics. "To my mind," he continues, "the spirit of Huss alone is in its proper place here."[1]

The Composer's Scheme for "Luther"

Schumann seems, indeed, from his correspondence with Pohl, to have formulated a well-defined scheme, and one which, had it come to fruition, might have resulted in a work both striking and original. The purposed oratorio was to be as suitable for church as concert-room. Two and a half hours' duration, including intervals, was the amount of time which it was to occupy in performance. Anything of a narrative or reflective nature was to be avoided as much as possible, the dramatic element to be introduced in preference. Evidently Schumann purposed to restore oratorio to its pristine and probably future character, when it should be something between a sacred opera and a musical mystery or miracle play. He begged his librettist in particular to give him plenty of opportunity

[1] *See* this interesting letter in its entirety in the published collections.

for chorus work, instancing Handel's "Israel in Egypt" as a model which, in this respect, he wished to follow. He refers to the introduction of Catherine as furnishing a soprano part, and indicates that the third part of the work would be best for the celebration of the marriage. The Choral, "Ein' Feste Burg," he intended should furnish the great climax and be reserved for the final chorus. He speaks, when writing, of the difficulty to be contended with in dealing with too many secondary characters—evidently Pohl had submitted a skeleton plot with *dramatis personæ*—and he considered that the Choral would be more appropriate than portions of the German Mass. Luther's musicianship and his well-known devotion to the Divine Art were also to be borne in mind and gracefully referred to. Finally, Schumann agrees with his librettist that the whole should be endued with the national spirit of the Fatherland. Schumann's own earnestness and thorough grasp of his subject are apparent, and evidently Pohl was as ardent over the topic as his distinguished musician correspondent.

Librettist and Musician

But the pity is when librettist and composer are not unanimous as to the form which a text is to assume. Much letter-writing passed between the two. Pohl's idea was a kind of grand Reformation Trilogy, with which Schumann did not agree. The musician wanted what he called a distinctly "popular" oratorio, which all classes could appreciate, since Luther himself appealed to men of all kinds. In the September of the year Pohl called upon Schumann to personally discuss the "Luther" text. Yet, although the young author was anxious to please his distinguished collaborator, in January 1852 we still find Schumann looking forward to a book upon the Reformer. But the oratorio "Luther" was not to be. Again and again Schumann wrote to Pohl or instructed him upon special points, and repeatedly did Pohl try, but in vain, to fulfil the composer's wishes. 1851 to 1852—one of the last years of the composer's healthful activity—was passed in fruitless anticipation of what would certainly have given food for his genius. Such happenings, in the economy of life and art, are hard to be understood; just as it seems sad that Mozart, Schubert and Mendelssohn should have been cut off on the very threshold of their prime. In how far Pohl was remiss in supplying material for the book of words, it is impossible to say. He appears to have done his best, or, at least, tried honestly to do so. On the 27th December 1852 Schumann writes to him that, although ill for six months from a distressing complaint, he was far from giving "Luther" up and hoped his correspondent would not do so either. Even as late as March 1853 the musician wrote that he was still "deeply attached" to the "Luther" idea.

Further Compositions

One thing, at all events, Pohl did for the composer. He re-modelled, at considerable labour and trouble, Uhland's Ballad, "Des Sänger's Fluch"; and this, as Op. 139, Schumann subsequently set to music. Previously, about Christmas 1851, he had written an overture to Goethe's "Hermann and Dorothea." The Chemnitz poet, Moritz Horn, supplied him with material for "The Pilgrimage of the Rose" (Op. 112), the music to which was composed in the early summer of 1851. Indeed, this period proved a very fertile one, for to June of this year belongs another Ballad of Uhland's, "Der Königssohn" (Op. 116), set for *soli*, chorus and orchestra. This work appears to have specially interested the composer. So also did "The Pilgrimage of the Rose." Speaking of the first performance of the latter work in a note to Dr Klitzsch, Schumann refers to it as having made "a very agreeable impression on the audience." Other productions of this marvellously active brain at this time were musical settings of Geibel's "Vom Pagen und der Königstochter" (Op. 140) and Uhland's "Das Glück von Edenhall" (Op. 143).

Meeting with Brahms

Although the year 1853 was saddened by periods of mental depression and unmistakable signs of failing health, yet it was not altogether without its times of cheer and brightness. The tour to Holland, in company with his gifted wife, was very gratifying and encouraging to the composer. Another event, which, for the time, roused Schumann, was his meeting with and recognition of the genius of Brahms. This is the more remarkable as Johannes Brahms, being then only a youth of twenty, might naturally have appeared but an apprentice in musicianship to the matured master. But Schumann did not regard his junior fellow-artist in this light. Joachim had sent Brahms to him with a letter of friendly introduction. Schumann then heard Brahms play, and was powerfully struck, as much with the young man's ability as an executant as in regard to his gifts as a composer. With that keen insight of critical appreciation which he had shown in regard to Chopin, Berlioz and others, Schumann recognised in the youthful aspirant those qualities which were destined to make Brahms the man of mark among his fellow-musicians that he became. Consequently, with all that noble liberal-mindedness and freedom from bias and envy which so eminently characterised him, the elder tone poet at once hailed in the younger a brother bard fully equipped rather than one who had yet his badge of honour to win. Speaking of Brahms to Dr Härtel,[1] he characterises the newcomer as a young man who had deeply thrilled all with his marvellous music, and who was destined, without doubt, to make an immense stir in the musical world. Writing, on the same date, to Joachim, Schumann compares Brahms to a young eagle; to a grand river; to the Niagara "thundering down from the heights as a waterfall, bearing the rainbow in its waves, its banks courted by butterflies, and accompanied by nightingales' songs."[2] He further esteems Brahms as an apostle who should reveal many things which the Pharisees would be unable to comprehend for centuries. Indeed, for some considerable time after this memorable meeting, Schumann's letters are full of a wonderful enthusiam about young Brahms. After a silence of about nine years—once more the mysterious *nine*—the musician again assumed the *rôle* of critic, and wrote a remarkable article, entitled "Neue Bahnen" (New Paths), to introduce Brahms to the public. This essay appeared in the *Neue Zeitschrift* of 28th October 1853, the day after the last Düsseldorf concert which poor Schumann was able to conduct — though

[1] Letter, October 8, 1853. [2] Letter, October 8, 1853.

clearly in failing health—in its entirety. Ever generous and active in giving a helping hand where real merit or earnestness displayed itself, our Master Musician exerted himself successfully in obtaining an introduction to, and good terms for his works from, the famous music publishers, Messrs Breitkopf & Härtel (of Leipzig), for the youthful composer. Thus, almost with the expiring spark of that wonderful ardour and energy which so characterised his life exertions, Schumann bestirred himself to aid another to gain a footing upon the slippery ladder of fame which he himself had mounted so bravely, almost unaided and unappreciated.

Last Yearning Vienna-wards

Partly owing to the restlessness occasioned by his serious state of health, and partly no doubt due to that innate hypersensitiveness which keenly felt the want of delicacy and tact displayed by a certain section in Düsseldorf in endeavouring to supplant him in his duties as conductor, Schumann for many months contemplated a move to Vienna. A strange fascination still attracted him to the home of Haydn, Mozart, Schubert and Beethoven, in spite of the fact that the Viennese had failed, on more than one occasion, to give himself due appreciation.[1] At the close of 1852 he definitely expressed to Van Bruyck a wish to go and settle in Vienna if

[1] *See* page 37, *et. seq.* He had written, on May 10th, 1852, to Van Bruyck as follows: "All that you tell me about Vienna I had noticed myself in former years. And yet something always draws me back again, as though the spirits of the departed great ones were still visible, and as though Vienna were Germany's true musical home." (See *Letters.*)

any position as conductor opened up there for him. That the desire to migrate Viennawards had become a resolve, proved certain towards the close of 1853. He mentions to Joachim that he had received an indirect offer from "a certain town" wherein he and his wife had long wished to live;[1] and also, about the same time, he tells Van Bruyck that he hoped soon to be nearer to him. The winter of 1854-1855 is even named as the time when the Schumanns purposed going to Vienna, as Schumann himself quaintly puts it, to free themselves from the narrowness of life in a small town and for "change of air."

"Valley of the Shadow"

But Heaven had willed it otherwise. The coming of Brahms, for a while, drove the gloomy broodings from the composer's soul. In company with the youthful *maestro* and Dietrich,[2] Schumann had written a Pianoforte and Violin Sonata as a greeting to their mutual "beloved and honoured friend, Joseph Joachim." It was almost his latest musical effort—this portion of a work penned by three as a tribute to one whom they mutually admired and esteemed.[3] Ere long, fits of terrible depression would seize Schumann. Sometimes he fancied he heard the incessant sounding of one note; on other occasions strange harmonies haunted him and distracted his rest and peace. One night he dreamed that the spirits of Mendelssohn and Schubert appeared to him and gave him a theme. He afterwards tried to work up the subject thus mysteriously given, but he never completed this,

[1] Letter, November 1853. [2] Hofcapellmeister at Oldenburg.
[3] In a MS. in Herr Joachim's possession.

practically his last, composition.[1] At length, on February 27, 1854, a sad incident occurred. In one of his "mortal agonies of mind" the unhappy composer left his home and was seen to throw himself into the Rhine. He was rescued and brought back to his distressed and sorrowing family, and for a little while he rallied in spirits. But the awful depression of mind kept recurring at intervals, and even the sufferer himself expressed a wish that he should be placed in an asylum. That painful expedient at length became a necessity; and so, for two years, with temporary returns to his former self, Robert Schumann was under the care of Dr Richarz, at Endenich, near Bonn.

Release at Last

The pathos of genius thus blasted in its full prime must have been heartrending for those near and dear who were obliged to witness it. It is not for biographer or reader to linger long over the contemplation of such a sad and trying period. A merciful release came finally on July 29, 1856, when, in the arms of his faithful and noble wife, the harassed spirit at last broke free from its fleshly prison. Schumann was but forty-six when he died. He was buried at Bonn. Some seventeen years later, in August 1873, a great "Schumann Festival" was held in that town, the proceeds of which were devoted towards erecting a monument[2] over the grave of the deceased musician. Thus now, in the birthplace of Beethoven, whose genius he so keenly appreciated and admired—and close to the fair Rhine which he

[1] Brahms afterwards utilised this "spirit" theme in his Variations for Four Hands (Op. 23), a work dedicated to Schumann's daughter, Julie.
[2] Executed by Donndorf of Stuttgart.

loved so well, and beneath the waters of which he had almost found a grave—a beautiful trophy of the sculptor's art marks the last resting-place of Schumann.

"The End is not yet"

If a cloud obscured his powers in the hour of his maturity, and if silence fell all too suddenly where rare melody and richest harmonic combinations had reigned supreme, at least Schumann lived to make an indelible mark in the musical world, and to leave behind him the imperishable achievements of a great mind truly remarkable and unique. In his life, if he yielded too much at times to a morbid romanticism, he was always actuated by a lofty spirit of wholesome enterprise and exertion. In his writings he strove to inculcate the noblest and most straightforward of sentiments; and his entire freedom from envy and malice towards fellow-workers, as his sympathy and kindliness to the young and struggling, made him a man among men. Reticent and reserved, for the most part, in converse with his fellow-creatures, through the medium of music Schumann had an unrestrained channel whereby he could pour forth the inner and most sacred thoughts of his soul. That his marvellous tone forms and colouring should not appeal to all is no more to be wondered at than that the deepest and most earnest emotions of our natures, if demonstrated in unsympathetic surroundings, often bring upon us but the apathy and misunderstanding of those in whose powers of insight and appreciation we place most faith. But no grand impulse, no heart-whole effort, is ever quite in vain. Schumann had a message to give, and he gave it—fearlessly, tenderly and effectively. He was more than a mere musician; he was a poet and philosopher. In his letters—the mirror of his soul—his essays, and his musical compositions we get a fuller glimpse of his mind than any narrative of his life could give us. Let us turn, then, to these; and from the creative output of this great tone poet's soul learn what a noble resolve, coupled to remarkable gifts, may accomplish, even when the path is beset with difficulties and the close is apparent failure and collapse.

Schumann : The Man

CHAPTER VIII

Circumstances and the Man—The Short-lived Melodists—The Musician as Letter-writer—Published Letters—Classification of the Schumann Letters—To his Mother—Hypersensitiveness to Trouble—Maternal Letters—Letter Reference to Early Compositions—Correspondence with College Friends.

WE now come to consider Schumann, the man. With much sympathy, with deepest veneration, with tenderest solicitude, let us raise the veil that shrouds the soul of Schumann, the tone genius; and, while we wonder at the revelation, let us reverence and esteem.

Robert Schumann, the child, grew up, in comparatively unmusical surroundings, with music in his soul. From his earliest years he played and composed. In his teens he was strangely drawn to literature, discovering in romantic poetry a reflex of some of his many, even to himself, incomprehensible thoughts. In early manhood his creative yearnings were overshadowed by maternal opposition to his adoption of music as a profession, and by the struggle he was obliged to go through before he could claim as his wife the woman of his choice. Later, even upon the accomplishment of his fondest hopes and desires,

Circumstances and the Man

the incessant strain of editorial and musical output told upon a sensitive temperament and a frame not over robust. To such a spirit as Schumann's—tender, refined and poetic—the wear and tear of daily life, and the inevitable contact with a world mainly hard and self-seeking, were influences which threw him back upon himself, and caused him to live apart—a reserved and taciturn, but by no means soured or "unapproachable," man.

Short-lived Melodists

The *creative musician* is strangely constituted. The music that is within, while it inspires, often burns and sears. The brilliant, flashing steel may even wear out the scabbard before its time. When coupled with romanticism, and unsalted by the sterner qualities of giant endurance such as Bach and Handel possessed, music ofttimes rends soul from body long before the "threescore years and ten." It is strangely pathetic to mark that three of the greatest composers whom the world has ever seen—Mozart, Schubert and Mendelssohn—died young. With the two former the struggle for existence may have told upon otherwise strong *physiques;* with the latter no such excuse can be pleaded. If Haydn and Spohr lived to be old men, Weber and Chopin "passed" on the threshold of their prime. Schumann saw but his forty-sixth year. His fruition—owing to circumstances which were unavoidable—was late. Scarcely did he reach his maturity period when blight fell upon the golden harvest-field. It is not for mortals to say, "Oh, the pity of it!" We need but remember that "the end is not yet." Beyond the veil of flesh surely the light will be clear.

Musician as Letter-writer

Schumann was a great and gifted letter-writer. In his epistles, rather than in speech, he poured forth his heart. From these missives, then—written to relatives, acquaintances and strangers—may we best gather what kind of man our Master Musician was and what he aspired to be. If we want confirmation of this statement, it is only necessary to recollect what *she* says who understood Schumann best of all. We refer to those touching words of Madame Clara Schumann herself with regard to his early correspondence. "These letters," writes the distinguished wife of a gifted husband, "form a beautiful and touching memorial, revealing all the treasures of an ideal youthful nature, strong and energetic, and filled with the highest aims and aspirations." [1]

Published Letters

Up to the present time the letters of Schumann which have been published are contained in the two collections to which we have frequently referred, namely, the *Early Letters* and *The Life of Robert Schumann told in His Letters*, both ably translated into English from the original German by May Herbert. Numerous other letters of great interest still remain unpublished, and some of these, through the courtesy of friends, the writer has been privileged to see and quote. The space limits will, however, only permit the briefest summary of some of the most salient points of this interesting and really remarkable correspondence.

If an attempt were made to classify roughly all the

[1] Preface by Madame Clara Schumann to *Early Letters of Robert Schumann* (translated by May Herbert).

CLARA SCHUMANN, *née* WIECK.

Schumann letters now available for perusal, perhaps the following order of consideration would give the best idea of the variety of style, freedom and reserve which we may expect to find in the whole series. First are the youthful letters; particularly those to his mother, his guardian, Herr Rudel, and his college acquaintances, Rosen and Götte. In the second category would come, perhaps, those emotional letters of early manhood to sympathetic friends, such as Henriette Voigt; and, as a great addenda to this division we must include the wonderful epistolary chats of his "love period," when the scribe raised the curtains of his inmost soul to Clara Wieck, the noble artist who afterwards became his loving wife and true helpmeet. Thirdly, there are groups of letters to students, fellow-workers, publishers, and, notably, to famous contemporary musicians—the latter being particularly interesting to the *connoisseur*. Under a miscellaneous heading we might place the purely business letters (though these were by no means prosaic), as also the many characteristic communications with strangers, outsiders, and admirers generally with whom Schumann was brought in touch through one circumstance or another.

Classification of the Schumann Letters

How deeply Schumann revered his mother, and how keenly her nature and his could enter into the thoughts and aspirations of each other, is more than evident, especially in those early letters written by the youth when a student at the Leipzig University. Imbued, as he was at the time, with the melancholy romanticism of Jean Paul, and striving in the dark for those repressed musical powers which it almost seemed a filial duty to keep in abeyance, a letter written from Leipzig, and dated August 31, 1828, may be referred to as characteristic and tending to throw a strong searchlight upon the mind of the dreamer, poet and musician. In this the youth of eighteen speaks of his life as being "monotonous and *joyless*." Thus early had morbid feelings taken possession of him. He continues that it gives him little pleasure to go about in public, and that it worries him to meet with silly folk. Music, however, he says, supplies the void to him which the outside world cannot fill. His piano whispers to him the thoughts he cannot put in words. When sad and lonely he thinks of the loved ones at home, and of the pleasant country places—the Weissenborn meadows, the Bankenberg, and Oberhohndorf—where, as a child, he so often wandered, full of blissful dreams. Pondering over those things he is both glad and sad, and feels as though he could weep. "Ah, mother," he concludes, "I have too soft a nature, I feel that; and every creature who feels so deeply must be unhappy."[1]

Schumann's Letters to his Mother

That this somewhat brooding and melancholy spirit was inherited seems evident from the many little appeals which he makes to his mother to write brighter letters. Doubtless the more hopeful and sanguine temperament of his father inspired the lad when, in a subsequent letter,[2] he proceeds to remonstrate tenderly and almost playfully with his mother to be more cheerful and not to lose the heaven-bestowed gifts of life through want of proper enjoyment and appreci-

[1] *Early Letters.* [2] Early letter, October 24, 1828.

ation of them. A year later he chides her gently for being sad, and bids her look out upon Nature and be happy, adding, "Why, indeed, can you not *enjoy* your happiness as much as you *deserve* to do?" [1]

Hypersensitiveness to Trouble

The fact was that, so sensitive was the highly-strung mind of the young poet-musician that he shrank from all that jarred or interrupted the harmony of his own vivid musings. In an ordinary nature the disinclination to allow himself to be upset by the troubles of others might have appeared selfishness or hyper-self-solicitude. In Schumann's case one must recollect that the musician's nervous temperament was developed in him to an extent that rendered him peculiarly vulnerable by discords literal and figurative—grievances real and fancied. Hence we are not surprised to hear him confess that he kept a letter of his mother's unread for a week when he perceived the gloomy frame of mind in which it started. He could not bear even to be told of sickness and death in his family.[2] "I have never before known sorrow," he writes, "now it has come upon me, but I cannot get over it, and it has crushed me a thousandfold." [3] At the time of writing this, however, the composer himself was recovering from a severe illness.

But it should not be conjectured from the above that his mother always, or even often, wrote to her absent son in a melancholy or morbid strain. Her letters, which seem to

[1] Early Letter, December 4, 1829.

[2] In this connection musicians will remember how keenly Mendelssohn felt the news of the death of his sister Fanny, a sad happening which, many believe, hastened his own end.

[3] Early Letter, January 4, 1834.

have come to Schumann with much frequency during his university career, appear to have been highly appreciated and cherished by him. He speaks of them being as intellectual as herself—"a lovely crystal mirror of your soul, which lights up and warms your son's heart." On one occasion he writes to tell her how much her recent letters had brightened and comforted him. He then refers to her "self-sacrificing love," which he had, at times, perhaps misunderstood. Sleeping or waking, he says, he seems to see her stand before him as his good genius, "always gentle and loving, and as though transfigured by youth."[1]

Maternal Letters

It is quaint to hear him beg her, in another letter, with his poet's conception of all that was dainty and beautiful, to write upon better notepaper! Then he reminds her that he always liked to see her well dressed, in her white lace cap and black silk gown, and could not endure the sight of her old grey one. It is a charming, affectionate letter, more like what a loving daughter would write than a young student, whatever his profession. But youth just entering manhood is all there, and must have made his proud mother smile when she read his postscript:—"*Apropos*. Don't be frightened! I am growing a moustache."

But for the full and very entertaining correspondence—such of it as has been preserved—that passed from this devoted son to an equally devoted mother, we must refer the reader to those *Early Letters*, from the English version of which such quotations as we have made have been taken.

Letter Reference to Early Compositions

[1] Early Letter, March 19, 1834.

Occasionally, but not often, Schumann speaks of his musical attainments to his mother. When in Leipzig, about the summer of 1834, Gottfried Weber had written an interesting criticism of the "Papillons" and some other early works. In this the writer had spoken of the young artist, Herr Schumann, who emitted "fiery sparks somewhat early." Weber had, however, highly commended the work and prophesied future success for the composer, although he animadverts upon the straining to be "extraordinary and original." This notice the young composer sent to his mother with his own unique and highly perspicuous comments. He was evidently pleased, and not a little flattered, by the verdict, such as it was, and speaks of it as coming from "our greatest critic." But he defends himself with all the confidence of genius. "They" (the "Papillons"), he says, "are anything but ultra-original; and I am inclined to question whether we young artists (Chopin, Hiller, etc.) have not rather more genius than they give us credit for, when the word is applied to things we have known and done with for ages." [1]

Correspondence with College Friends

Of youthful letters, full of great thoughts and aspirations for the future, few are so entertaining as those written to his college friend, Rosen, to whom he was deeply and sincerely attached. In these, more than in any others, perhaps, of his communications, we see the trend of the young student's thoughts when life, with all its mysteriousness and solemnity, was just opening up to him. One letter in particular,

[1] Early Letter, written from Leipzig, July 2, 1834.

that to his chum, William Götte, is well worth perusal. In this we see Schumann the dreamer striving for the indefinable *something* which means the great ideal of the earnest-minded man. He distinguishes between the *epic* and *lyric* nature, claiming to belong to the latter himself. Thus, to him, music, the twilight, the sunrise, all arouse in him the yearning for a greater, higher phase of energy and existence. Schumann the philosopher and seer, perhaps, speaks when he writes:—"We can scarcely imagine the great unfinished picture of man in *space*; but in *time* the titanic giant spirits join hands for the formation of the highest, and for the gigantic work of completed creation."[1]

[1] Letter to William Götte, written from Schneeberg, October 2, 1828.

CHAPTER IX

Madame Henriette Voigt—Ernestine Von Fricken—Susceptibility to Feminine Grace and Sympathy—The Poet-Musician and Beauty—Friendship for Robena Laidlaw—First Meeting with Schumann—A Stroll in the Rosenthal—Subjects of Conversation—Jansen's and Wenzel's Tributes to the Composer's Early Conversational Powers—Youthful Sociability—The Attainments and Personal Charm of Robena Laidlaw—Two Hitherto Unpublished Letters.

THUS far have we glimpses of Schumann, the youthful aspirant. Tinctured, as he confessedly was, with the sentimentality of Jean Paul, there is, nevertheless, a sanguinity of impulse and endeavour which is pre-eminently *Schumannesque* and nobly resolute in this pouring forth of his most sacred yearnings. As he verged into manhood, and was gradually drawn, almost unconsciously, into a social circle of young people of his own age, and of sympathetic natures akin to his, the more ecstatic fibres of his being were thrilled to expression; and, in many fervid letters to his early friends, notably of the other sex, we see manifestations of a gentle, refined, and yet exultant spirit that was deeply moved by the beauty, grace and talent of several fair and gifted women who came within the group of his acquaintances.

Schumann's early friendship for Madame Henriette Voigt has already been noticed. This charming woman entered thoroughly into the musical and poetic yearnings of the young man; and it is evident from their correspondence—Schumann made her his confidant in regard to his passing fancy for Ernestine Von Fricken—that Madame Voigt took a kindly and sisterly interest in him, and, with refined womanly instinct, wished to see him happily married. Writing to her in the summer of 1834, the composer refers to the spiritual and musical affinity that existed between them, and discloses his own strange sensitiveness and reserve by confessing that her kind expressions of sympathetic concern for him sometimes drew him out and sometimes caused him to shrink within himself, after the manner of polar attraction and repulsion.[1] Through the years that followed Schumann did not forget this early friend, and several letters passed between them with regard to his work and hopes for the future. One of the last of these communications, written in the autumn of 1839, speaks of having got her letter late at night, and, although it was dark, knowing who it came from. He tells her how he has noticed that, in Berlin, nearly everyone appears to be fond of reading, whereas in Vienna they think more of eating. Then he speaks of hearing very little music, adding that it was perhaps better so, as he only cared for the best, and found his greatest comfort and encouragement in Bach. He then refers briefly to his own compositions of the time, and hopes that the publishers may soon bring out his Sonata[2] dedicated to her "as a sign of old affec-

Madame Henriette Voigt

[1] Letter to Henriette Voigt, July 3, 1834.
[2] Sonata No. 2, in G minor (Op. 22).

tion." Concluding, he sends greetings to her husband and little daughter, Ottilie, "with her great blue eyes," adding that these latter just suited his "Kinderscenen." The last sentences of the letter [1] are significant. He bids his friend good-bye, begs her to take care of herself, and hopes that they may meet soon again. Two months afterwards Madame Voigt [2] was no more.

Ernestine von Fricken

Arising out of his intimacy with the Voigt musical family came another friendship of a still more romantic character. We have spoken of his profession of love for, and brief engagement with, the amateur pianist, Baroness Ernestine von Fricken, to whom, in 1831, he inscribed his "Allegro" (Op. 8). Those who are acquainted with the composer's "Carnaval," know that it is largely based on four letters, A.S.C.H., and their transposition, S.C.H.A. The former spelt the birthplace of the young lady referred to, and the latter were the musical letters in Schumann's own name.[3] Schumann had a great vein of superstition in him, and was much affected by impressions, coincidences and the like. In a touching and almost reverential letter which he wrote to Ernestine, before he had definitely become betrothed to her, he speaks of his good genius having brought them together in a kind of external relationship.[4] "I am too modest," he says, "to think you would care to acknowledge a deeper, more artistic, mental relationship."[5] In closing the letter he expresses his deepest devotion, and wishes that time might

[1] Letter to Madame Henriette Voigt, August 11, 1839.

[2] *See* page 20.

[3] *See* also page 186.

[4] They had both been sponsors to one of Wieck's children.

[5] Early Letter, July 28, 1834.

stand still, probably that he might continue in his then happy frame of mind.

Suscepti-bility to Feminine Grace and Sympathy

That Schumann was in earnest about this early attachment we can scarcely doubt. To their mutual friend, Madame Voigt, he declared that Ernestine's love was a heaven-sent gift to him. It is not for us to speculate as to why this little romance so soon resolved itself into dust and ashes. Nor can we allow any suspicion of fickleness to attach to the name of Schumann. Here again his susceptible and deeply emotional nature must be taken into account. For him to meet with tenderness and sympathy, especially when it was combined with talented and attractive womanhood, meant that his heart was stirred rather with an affectionate yearning for the unattainable, than with an unreasoning and transient passion for a beautiful face. For one so prone to human kindliness and grace in others as was Schumann, it was impossible to let such pass by without his warmest tribute of appreciation, and even devotion. His spirit was essentially a loving and lovable one, and thus we can well understand that, until he realised the strength and power which alone could fully satisfy him in the heroic yet gentle nature of Clara Wieck, he could ill refrain from pouring forth his feelings under the influence of kind eyes or tender words of appreciation and fellow-feeling. Even to Clara herself, when they were engaged, the lover unfolds this trait of his mind. In one communication, while bewailing his habitual coldness and reserve, which often made the best-intentioned friends misunderstand him, he speaks of feeling very deeply the least display of kindness, and being stirred by even a look or the almost imperceptible softening of other natures towards him. "For I have not got a bad heart," he says naïvely, "and love all that is good and beautiful with my whole soul." [1]

On a previous occasion he had confessed to his betrothed that he had many faults, though they were growing less than formerly. Their having to wait so long before marriage, he continues, had at least the advantage that they should gain a better experience of each other—a knowledge that often came only after marriage to other people. The "faults" that Schumann then acknowledges were his fondness for showing his affection for the people he loved by playing tricks on them, and his admiration for beautiful women. Then he playfully begs his *fiancée* not to be distressed or to scold him if, some day they are out walking together and they meet somebody really pretty, he should exclaim, "Oh, Clara, look at that divine creature!" [2]

Poet-Musician and Beauty

We now come to Schumann's meeting with, and friendship for, Miss Robena Laidlaw (the late Mrs Thomson), the gifted pianist, who is mentioned in the *Life of Louis Berger* as one of his most famous pupils. Anna Robena [3] came of an old and highly-respected family that had once owned large landed property in the south of Scotland. The

[1] Early Letter to Clara Wieck, written from Vienna, December 29, 1838.
[2] Early Letter, April 13, 1838.
[3] The order of the lady's names was Robena Anna Laidlaw, but Schumann himself suggested the transposition to *Anna Robena* as being more "musical."

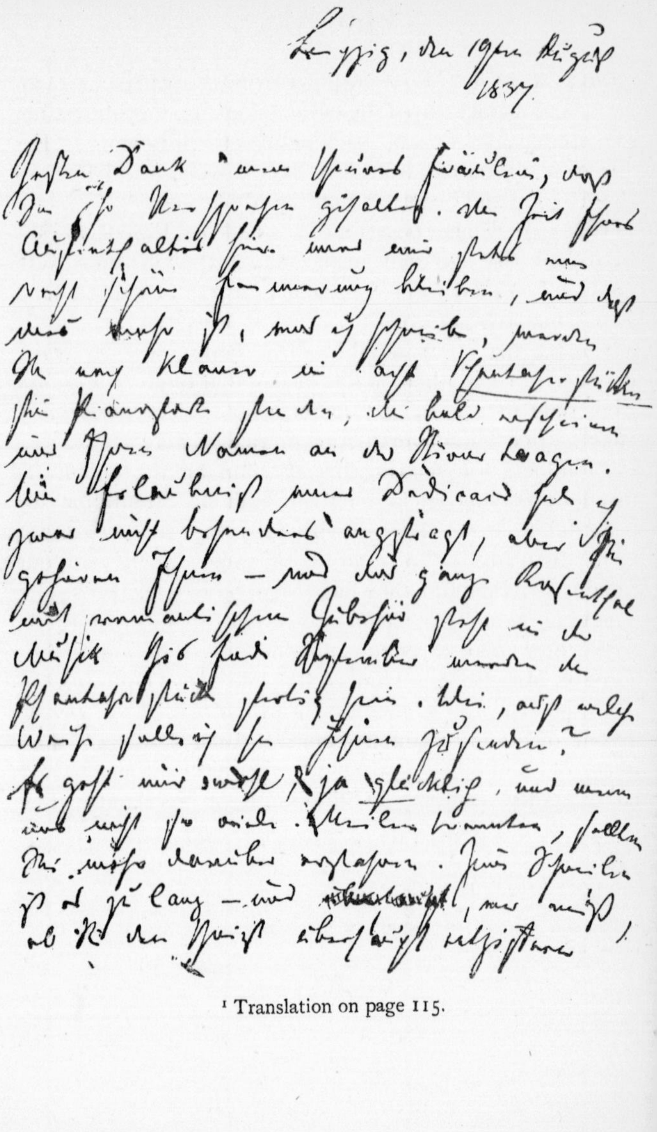

Leipzig, den 19ten August
1837.

Besten Dank, mein theures Fräulein, dass
Sie Ihr Versprechen gehalten. Die Zeit Ihres
Aufenthaltes hier wird eine stete mir
recht schöne Erinnerung bleiben, und dass
dies wahr ist, was ich schreibe, werden
Sie nach [illegible] in acht Phantasiestücken
für Pianoforte finden, die bald erscheinen
mit Ihrem Namen an der Stirne tragen.
Um Erlaubniss zur Dedication hab ich
zwar nicht besonders angefragt, aber sie
gehören Ihnen — und der ganze Rosenthal
mit romantischem Zubehör steht in der
Musik. Bis Ende September werden die
Phantasiestücke fertig sein. Wie, auf welche
Weise soll ich sie Ihnen zusenden?
Es geht wohl direct, ja gleichzeitig, und wenn
man nicht so viele Meilen trennten, sollen
Sie mehr darüber erfahren. Ihr Schreiben
ist oft zu lang — und [illegible], wer weiss,
ob Sie der Schrift überhaupt entziffern!

[1] Translation on page 115.

Kummer, so große Mühe ich mir auch gegeben
habe und eben gebe, mich zu zeigen.
(Mich zu zeigen, ist wirklich lobbar.) —
Hr. Anger ist erstaunlich nachsinnend ge-
worden nach Ihrer Abreise und er
schwärmt oft einen ganzen Tag jeden Abend
im Hotel de Baviere. Die Quartette
verschiebt sich Ihnen.
Ihr Lied habe ich bis jetzt noch nicht
erhalten. Sie werden es nicht vergessen,
überhaupt?
Schreiben Sie mir von Ihren kleinen
Studien; Sie glauben nicht, wie sehr
ich Theil nehme an Allem. Lindenberg
ist breit. Gehen Sie noch dahin?
Empfehlen Sie mich Ihrem vortrefflichen Hrn.
Müller, der so lebendig vor mir steht,
mit Ihrem ganzen Natur
und geben Sie bald ein Zeichen
der Erinnerung
Ihrem
ergebenen
Robert Schumann

Antworten Sie mir
lieber in englischer
Sprache, ich bitte
recht schön darum

Laidlaws had been on very intimate terms with Sir Walter Scott, Robena's grandmother having once made a cap for the great novelist, which he habitually wore when writing, and which he used to call his "wishing cap."[1] At an early age Robena had shown marked musical talent, and, when studying in Germany, had placed herself, at the advice of Rellstab (one of Schumann's friends), under the tuition of Louis Berger. Rellstab spoke very highly of her beautiful touch and tone and interpretative powers (she was then but fourteen years of age), and Berger seems to have been much attached to her and to have thought most highly of her playing. Later on she performed with great success before the Court at Berlin; in the presence of English royalty in London; obtaining the most flattering of all receptions from the imperial circle in Russia. In Vienna, Paris, Brussels, and indeed all the chief art centres of Europe, Miss Laidlaw invariably delighted and charmed all who heard her, receiving jewels from numerous Courts, and being warmly and enthusiastically complimented by crowned heads, as by famous artists of the day like Paganini, etc.[2]

Friendship for Robena Laidlaw

But there was more than mere virtuosity about Robena Laidlaw. In a most interesting account, by Professor Jansen,

[1] This old Mrs Laidlaw referred to told Sir Walter Scott of the existence of the creature—a real personage—who afterwards gave name to the romance of *The Black Dwarf*.

[2] Paganini, writing of Miss Laidlaw's playing at his farewell concert, says, "I shall never forget the prodigious effect she produced at my concert, and confess never to have heard that instrument (the piano) treated so magnificently."

First Meeting with Schumann

of her meeting with Robert Schumann,[1] we are told of her "charming and modest personality and great beauty," as of "the delicacy and sympathy of her style," and her "strength and *bravura*" in rendition. At the time when she met Schumann her artistic gifts were beginning to bring her into prominence, and in appearance and temperament she had inherited the beautiful eyes and lively disposition of her Irish mother. Such was the brilliant young girl when, in 1837, having obtained an introduction to him, she called one morning upon Schumann, accompanied by Mrs Laidlaw and one Herr Fürstenau (a brother of the celebrated flautist of that name in Dresden). The interview is best told in Miss Laidlaw's own words :—

"As I entered Schumann's sitting-room," she writes, "I was struck by its simplicity and want of ostentation. He was in a dressing-gown, seated at his writing-table and smoking a cigar. At first he appeared slightly embarrassed at being found in this attire, but very soon, having presented our conductor to him, we entered into most friendly conversation, and, indeed, remained there a considerable time. Among the furniture of the room the one thing I remember distinctly was a grand piano, but I am not very observant of details and my whole attention at the time was fixed upon the very distinguished and unaffected man we were visiting. Schumann was kindness itself, spoke of my artistic success in Warsaw, and said, in taking leave, that he would soon

[1] "Robert Schumann and Robena Laidlaw," by Professor Jansen. Article published in 1895 in the *Grenzboten*.

return our visit, which, in fact, he did (if I remember rightly) the same afternoon. We laughed about a mistake he made as to the identity of the gentleman who accompanied us. Knowing I had just returned from Warsaw, and not catching exactly the name Fürstenau, Schumann was under the impression that our escort was 'Ein Fürst aus Warsau' (a prince from Warsaw)."

A Stroll in the Rosenthal

Schumann then heard Miss Laidlaw play pieces by different composers, and expressed himself exceedingly pleased with her remarkable interpretative powers in various styles. He at once undertook to help her with her forthcoming concert, and secured for her the valuable assistance of David, of the celebrated baritone, Hammermeister (creator of the part of the Templar in Marschner's opera) and others, as well as drawing special attention in his paper to the remarkable gifts and attainments of the young English *pianiste.* Subsequently the Laidlaw ladies—mother and daughter—saw a good deal of him. On one occasion he escorted them to the Rosenthal (Valley of Roses). "The weather," writes Miss Laidlaw, "was beautiful, and we three wandered about the gardens. After coffee I proposed a walk round the place. We had hardly started when Schumann suddenly left us and hurried to a little hillock. While my mother and I waited for his return we noticed him examining minutely every rose bush on the path, always shaking his head and then going further on. At last, at the top of the mound, he stopped, and having carefully examined a rose tree, cut off a blossom. Coming down the hill very quickly, he handed it to me, remarking that he had looked in vain among the trees for a rose without spot or blemish fit to offer me, and had at last only then found one on which even the green leaves were perfect. I thanked him, and then he suggested a row on the lake. My mother would not venture on the water and was rather against my doing so, but remarking Schumann's disappointment I said I was quite ready to go under his care. He then secured a boat, arranged the cushions, and we started, leaving my mother sitting at the water side. He rowed very well, and sometimes drew my attention to the pretty surrounding scenery, or else conversed on other subjects, always intellectually and with charm. After an hour's delightful row we returned to my mother, and then we all three had a pleasant walk together." Schumann, Miss Laidlaw adds, was very fond of these rowing expeditions and often repeated the pleasure.

Subjects of Conversation

Referring to Schumann's conversation, Miss Laidlaw remarks that it was "always spiritual and fascinating—in fact, entirely original, for he never copied anyone either in manner or words." Hoffmann was often mentioned, of whom the composer seemed very fond. He was also a great admirer of Sir Walter Scott and his works, and was much interested to hear how intimate the famous poet and novelist had been with the young pianist's grandparents—the Laidlaws of Glenrath and Chapelhope. Sterndale Bennett was also frequently referred to; in fact, Bennett, who had previously been much struck with Miss Laidlaw's talent, had written to Schumann of her as "a kind of wonder," and had asked the composer to help her in every way he could.

"Once," continues Miss Laidlaw, "we were talking of Raphael's Madonna in Dresden, and Schumann said his idea of the Madonna was that she should be half child, half woman. His own favourite picture was Murillo's Madonna in the Louvre." When discussing various musicians and singers of the time, Miss Laidlaw remarks that she never heard Schumann malign or belittle any artist, nor did she ever observe in him anything approaching taciturnity or ill-humour. "Of Schumann's manners and character," proceeds Miss Laidlaw, "we formed the impression that he was, in every sense of the word, a *gentleman*, and absolutely devoid of any little vanity or self-importance." He seems, indeed, to have been courtesy itself to the two English ladies. One evening he took them to the theatre to hear Hammermeister sing. Miss Laidlaw noticed he had a deep red carnation in his hand. After much hesitation he at length handed it to her, saying, "Bitte nehmen sie diese Blume" (Please accept this flower). "He was, indeed, full of German kind-heartedness and simplicity," remarks the lady, in reference to this little incident, "and I have never met an artist, Paganini perhaps excepted, who could approach him in true modesty both as composer and as man. In some ways he recalled my honoured teacher, Louis Berger, whose manners were like his—simple, straightforward, and without any pretensions."

Professor Jansen, in his article referred to, "Robert Schumann and Robena Laidlaw," to which we are indebted for much of the above interesting information, adds a note to the effect that Miss Laidlaw's description of Schumann's kindliness and geniality of manner and address, which accords exactly with that of Wenzel, shows that the composer's taciturnity, of which so much was said during his later years, did not exist to any great extent in his younger days. Jansen himself (who is undoubtedly one of the foremost of Schumann authorities) has said that Schumann could be very chatty. Wenzel also told Jansen that, when in his talkative moods, the composer had discussed "everything under the sun" with him.[1]

Jansen's and Wenzel's Tributes

Nor does it appear from the reminiscences of the late Mrs Thomson (*née* Robena Laidlaw) that Schumann was by any means a recluse, or eschewed social gatherings or the companionship of fellow-artists. He seems to have taken the Laidlaw ladies about a good deal, and to have introduced them to his friends. In this way they were frequent guests at the hospitable house of the Frieses, who were on very intimate terms with the composer; and the Brockhaus[2] family also made the acquaintance of Robena through Schumann, and thought very highly of her, giving a dinner in her honour. After Miss Laidlaw's concert at the Gewandhaus, the composer himself turned entertainer, and inaugurated a dinner to the heroine of the day at the Hotel de Bavière, inviting, among others, Dr Reuter, Walter von Goethe, Dr Monicke, Wenzel and Anger. Again, shortly before their departure from Leipzig, Schumann entertained the English ladies to supper at the same place. "As we returned late through

Youthful Sociability

[1] Wasielewski appears rather to have doubted the correctness of Jansen's statement. But the weight of personal testimony which we have been able to obtain goes to prove the fact that Schumann could be very bright and talkative in congenial surroundings.

[2] A sister of Richard Wagner married Brockhaus, the publisher.

the silent streets," writes Miss Laidlaw, "I remarked to Schumann, who was walking by me, that it reminded me somewhat of a Don Juan exploit. Herr Anger, who was immediately behind us, mumbled some words which no one could understand, but Schumann declared he was vexed because he was not walking by me, so I turned round from time to time to address a few friendly words to him."[1]

Robena Laidlaw

Shortly afterwards Miss Laidlaw left Leipzig. That Schumann esteemed the brilliant young artist highly seems evident. "I must especially congratulate you on having made the acquaintance of Herr Schumann," wrote Louis Berger to his pupil, "a very clever, critical genius"—at the time our subject was better known as an editor than a composer—"and he appears to be extraordinarily taken with your great musical talent." The Frieses also wrote to her, saying, "Schumann speaks very often of you." That Robena Laidlaw possessed rare charm of manner as of appearance all who ever met her will readily bear testimony. Wenzel always spoke of her as "*bildhubschen*" (girl beautiful as a picture). "It is easy," says Jansen, "to understand Anger's admiration for the beautiful young Englishwoman whose poetic and charming appearance attracted every eye." Even in her last days the artist rejoiced in excellent health, bodily and mental. "She is a very amiable lady," says Pauer, "of medium size, a beautiful complexion, most expressive eyes, very lively in conversation, taking interest in everything." Well does the writer remember being intro-

[1] *See* the letter from Schumann to Miss Laidlaw on pages 115-116.

duced to her a few years before her death. Surrounded by a happy circle of admiring friends and her gifted daughters, the late Mrs Thomson looked like a queen, and beamed upon all with that wonderful tenderness and sympathy which kept her ever young in heart. She had the rare gift of personal magnetism, which drew all to her. It lay partly in her glance. Probably she had inherited "the Irish eyes" of her mother, which Schumann had warmly admired.[1] There was in her voice also the faintest *soupçon* of the musical Munster dialect, just enough to stir the hearer with its fervour and enthusiasm, which age could not chill. One could have listened for hours to her account of the pleasant recollections of days gone by; but no reminiscence seemed so cherished by her as her meeting with, and being so kindly treated by, Schumann. Her judgment of the great composer is the more valuable as it was grounded upon her personal knowledge of him, and has been expressed in her letters with entire unconventionality. She passed away on May 29, 1901, full of years and honours.[2]

Such was the gifted lady for whom Schumann wrote, and to whom he dedicated, his wonderful "Fantasiestücke," known as "Opus 12." He thus writes of the group of pieces to Miss Laidlaw on August 19, 1837 :—

"Best thanks, my dear Fräulein, that you have kept your

[1] *See* page 117.

[2] The authoress is indebted to the late Mrs Thomson's daughter, Mrs Sophie Metcalfe (herself a distinguished pianist and most successful teacher of piano) for the above personal reminiscences, as also for permission to quote *in extenso* two letters of the composer (on pages 115-117) which have never hitherto been published. *See* also facsimile illustration.

Unpublished Letters

promise (to write). The time of your stay here will always be a most beautiful memory to me, and that this is true you will soon see in 8 "Phantasiestücke" for pianoforte that will shortly appear bearing your name upon their forehead. It is true I have not asked for permission to make this dedication, but they belong to you, and the whole 'Rosenthal,' with its romantic surroundings, is in the music. The "Phantasiestücke" will be ready by the end of September. How, and in what way, shall I send them to you? All goes well with me—yes, very well—and if so many miles did not separate us you should hear more about it. Writing is too long, and who knows if you will be able to decipher the letter, notwithstanding the pains I have taken, and am taking even now, to make it distinct. Herr Anger has become very absent-minded since your departure, and often raves about that June evening in the Hotel de Bavière. Dr Reuter begs to be remembered to you. I have not yet received your picture. You will not forget it, will you?

"Write to me about your plans, studies, etc. You cannot think how interested I am in all. Petersburg is a long way off—are you going there? Remember me to your honoured mother, whom I think I can see before me now, and also to your father; and give soon a sign that you remember your devoted

"ROBERT SCHUMANN.

"Please answer me in English. I should like that very much."

In a later letter to Miss Laidlaw, Schumann showed how

prettily and gracefully he could pay a charming compliment without being either fulsome or sentimental. Writing from Leipzig on September 8, 1837, he says:—

"HONOURED FRÄULEIN,—First of all in my name, and in those of all your friends here, give your father the heartiest thanks for the cigars. In my life, I swear to you, I have never seen any better. I sit like a god between the blessed clouds and murmur to myself, 'No, this is too good!' Now imagine to yourself all the rest.

"I have just received your picture and the drawings of the flowers. At a time when people promise so much which they do not fulfil, your attention has an elevating effect upon me. I thank you from my heart for all, and remain greatly your debtor. The picture is, however, unflattering in the highest degree. Where can one see something of the eyes as they are, and of the blue velvet bodice? Truly I value you more highly than the picture. I want to hear a great deal about you soon. What are you playing? What are your plans for the future? Is Leipzig entirely out of the question, and will you not soon come back to us?

"Let me have a line about all this, and soon. And, once more, I should like it to be in English.

"Remember me to your parents. The eyes of Mistress Laidlaw[1] I seem to see before me.—Your devoted

"ROBERT SCHUMANN."

[1] Schumann had said that the "Irish eyes" of Robena Laidlaw's mother were the most beautiful he had ever seen.

CHAPTER X

Clara Josephine Wieck—A Contemporary's Opinion upon Madame Schumann's Playing—Madame Schumann as Composer—Early Admiration—A Musician's Love-Letters—Madame Schumann as an Interpretative Artist—The Musician and his Children.

Clara Josephine Wieck

PASSING from this correspondence of friendship, and even admiration, we come to something stronger, deeper than all, in the life of the composer. We refer to his great love for Clara Wieck, which was faithful to her through years of trouble and unrest, through absence, and through trials of all kinds. When the composer first met Friedrich Wieck's famous daughter she was very young, little more than a child. But even then she was displaying talents, as a pianist, of a remarkable order. Clara Josephine Wieck, born in Leipzig, September 13, 1819, had commenced her musical studies at a very early age under her father, one of the foremost teachers of the day. She made her *début* as a pianist at the age of nine, and appeared at the Gewandhaus Concerts in October 1832, being then but thirteen, upon which occasion she played the solo part of Moscheles's G minor Concerto. At first she favoured *bravura* music; but, ere long, doubtless under the influence of Mendelssohn and Schumann, her tastes turned definitely and permanently to classic work of the highest order. Shortly before her husband's death, Madame Schumann visited England, and played at the Philharmonic Concerts on April 14 and 28, 1856. She was not heard in London again till the season of 1865, when her engagements at the Philharmonic Society and the Musical Union established her fame to such an extent in this country that subsequently her visits to the English metropolis became annual ones with but few intermissions. In 1878 this truly great and remarkable artist, having obtained European reputation, was appointed Professor of Pianoforte at the Frankfort Conservatoire, where many now famous pupils had the benefit of her instruction. Critical estimates of her skill as a pianist are numerous. Perhaps one of the best known is that admirable one of Mr Franklin Taylor, quoted in the able article on "Clara Schumann" in Grove's *Dictionary of Music and Musicians.*

A Contemporary's Opinion upon Mme. Schumann's Playing

In a brightly-written biography of Madame Amina Goodwin, a distinguished pupil of Madame Schumann, the author, Mr Algernon Rose—a foremost authority on the pianoforte and pianoforte playing—thus conveys the lady pianist's estimate of her famous instructress:—

"In Madame Schumann's playing, so deep, full and clear were the sounds produced that the two hands conveyed an impression that they were each possessed of five index fingers—the index finger being usually the strongest and most flexible of one's hand. Especially in slow and *cantabile* playing was this effect noticeable. By the method adopted it seemed as if the nerve bulbs at the end of each finger became abnormally sensitive, so deep was the touch when depressing each note. In rapid execution the runs were clear and even ; and in passages formed of notes of the same value throughout, so equal was the execution that there was no irregularity in lapse of time between the playing of each note. In putting forth complete strength, however great, the tone produced by Madame Schumann was never harsh nor hard. It remained mellow, deep, persuasive and sonorous. In very soft playing it was apparent that an endeavour was made to elicit the tone in such a manner from the instrument, by gently pressing into the keys, that the piano rang with resonance and carrying power. In this method the left hand was cultivated until competent to play all the loud and brilliant passages with the same strength and solicitude as the right hand, and, according to Chopin's idea of what ought to be, the left hand served as *chef d'orchestre* to the right. Further, the subtle charms of light and shade, the *chiaro-scura* of tone and expression, were accomplished in the left with equal precision as in the right, one part never unduly preponderating over the other. It was unity in the production of the sound which caused brilliancy."[1]

Mme. Schumann as Composer

Such, as a performer, was the gifted woman so closely connected with the career of the subject of our biography. Madame Schumann was more than a mere *virtuosa*. She had a good theoretical knowledge and much inventive skill. She composed quite a number of pianoforte pieces—as well as several gracefully-written songs—all characterised by a charm essentially their own. Most of these have been published. Among them we would draw special attention to the "Three Preludes and Fugues," which not only supply excellent *legato* work to the player, but also serve to show the scholarship, as well as the facile

[1] *Amina Goodwin*, a biographical sketch by Algernon S. Rose, author of *Talks with Bandsmen*, *How to Choose a Piano*, etc.

powers in handling the severer musical forms, of this remarkably talented artist.

That Schumann was early struck with admiration, nay, even reverence, for the talented girl pianist, was evident. For a time, when he was a pupil of Wieck, the two young people had lived under the same roof. At this period they probably saw a great deal of one another, and took mutual interest in each other's studies and practice. Perhaps one of the first letters that passed between them was that written in the New Year of 1832, when Schumann addressed the youthful artist as "Dear honoured Clara," and signs himself, *in friendship*, as "Fräulein C. W.'s warmest admirer."[1] Two years afterwards there appears to be the awakening of a deeper feeling. He speaks of finding himself at the piano when he thinks intently of her. She even suggests chords of the Ninth and the Thirteenth to him! He quotes the following chord as being her musical equivalent:—

Early Admiration

Then he speaks of her recent letter to him as being herself all over. He can picture her in it as she talks and laughs, "rushing from fun to earnest as usual, diplomatically play-

[1] Early Letter, February 1, 1832.

ing with your veil: in short, the letter was Clara herself—her double." Then he goes on, in his playful, merry, affectionate way, about music, his literary work, etc., and plies her with questions about herself. He concludes with, "Addio, carissima Clara, cara Clarissima!"[1]

As yet there had been no talk of marriage between them. At the time, indeed, Schumann was contemplating betrothing himself to the fair Ernestine von Fricken, an event which took place shortly afterwards; but the engagement was, ere long, terminated by mutual consent. In 1834 it should be borne in mind that Clara was in early girlhood, having but entered upon her fifteenth year. In 1836, however, all came to be fully arranged between the young couple themselves, and, save for the opposition of Father Wieck, there was nothing to mar their mutual happiness in loving each other. We would gladly enter into the wonderful "love-letters" that follow, but as these are best read in their entirety, and as they can easily be consulted by interested readers, both in the original German as in the English versions, we must be content with a general analysis of their nature and contents.

A Musician's Love-Letters

In the first place, these *billets-doux* have nothing whatsoever of sickly sentimentality about them. They are written in a straightforward, earnest spirit, and seem rather to be a colloquy of two kindred souls that beat as one than the fervid adoration of the lover who looks upon the woman of his choice as simply a beautiful toy. There is that remarkable letter in which Schumann tells his betrothed

[1] Early Letter, July 10, 1834.

of his "faults."[1] In the same epistle he speaks of being deeply touched by all that takes place in the world. In his own way he ponders over politics, literature and people, and then longs to describe his sentiments *in music.* "That," he says, "is why my compositions are sometimes difficult to understand." He then attempts to analyse his own feelings as a composer. To talk about it, he declares, he cannot, though the subject deeply occupies his thoughts. He warns his future wife that she will find him very serious sometimes, and may not know what to make of him. It is quaint to hear of him asking her beforehand not to watch him too closely when composing, or else it would drive him to desperation. In return he will undertake to listen very seldom at her door when she would be practising! "Well," he concludes, "we shall indeed lead a life of poetry and blossom, and we will play and compose together like angels, and bring gladness to mankind.

Correspondence of this kind is deeply interesting and instructive, and tends to show how *thorough* was the mutual understanding and tolerance of these two. Theirs was no rash and hasty love match which, upon marriage, was to end in speedy disillusionment through want of comprehension of each other's temperaments. On the contrary, we see, even in their courtship period, the growth between them of that tender affection, deep solicitude, and the determination to "bear and forbear" with each other which alone constitutes the love that is deathless, and the soul's devotion which outlives the most ardent protestations of passion. That Schumann looked upon his

[1] *See* page 105. [2] Early Letter, April 13, 1838.

wife as rather part of himself than a separate identity is apparent. Satisfied in his home surroundings and his work, he, latterly, did not care to face the world. But in Clara he possessed a willing and able medium whereby his musical thoughts could best obtain a hearing. Thus was this noble woman literally "a right hand" to her husband—devoted, earnest, conscientious, highly gifted, and yet wonderfully simple-minded and womanly wherewithal.

Madame Schumann as an Interpretative Artist

The playing of Madame Clara Schumann is still fresh in the memory of many who were privileged to hear her, as essentially full, rich and thorough, coupled with a clear and perfect technique. Her insight in interpretation, with regard to the meaning of composers, was as honest as it was convincing and striking. The soul of Clara Schumann, artist and woman, revolted from anything that was tawdry or unworthy. Thus, in a time of claptrapism and mere empty virtuosity, she invariably aimed at and maintained a high standard of purity in tone, perfect execution apart from mere display, and intelligent and thorough rendition of the spirit as the letter of the music she undertook to perform. Added to all this, Madame Clara Schumann's interpretations had distinct characteristics all her own, in which were truly delineated the loyalty, sincerity and womanliness of her nature. The opinion of Mr A. J. Hipkins—the greatest living authority on the history of keyed instruments—is one of the most valuable that the writer has had the privilege of receiving, especially as it is based on personal experience and intimacy. Speaking of Madame Schumann as an artist, Mr Hipkins says: "She was not a moon to Schumann, shining by reflected light, but an independent luminary, giving her own reproduction of Schumann's creations, and possibly differing from what, had he continued a pianist, he might have made authoritative himself."

The Musician and his Children

That Schumann made an exemplary son and ideal lover and husband there can be little doubt, if we read aright these early letters to those who drew forth his most tender sympathies. He who, towards the close of his career, seems to have avoided converse with strangers and the outside world as much as possible, never failed, as a father, to find delight in the family circle. Like his famous contemporary, Mendelssohn, Schumann entered with zest into the little ones' games, and became, when in their midst, as if one of themselves. He had also a pleasant, "jokey" way with him that the young folk never failed to appreciate. Thus, on one occasion, as his youngest daughter has described to the writer, he met the little people in the street and pretended not to know who they were—a little piece of "funning" on the part of their father which the children much enjoyed, but which was perhaps slightly misunderstood by one of his biographers.[1] Were oral proof wanting to confirm this, there is the fact that, even in the zenith of his powers as a creative artist, the composer wrote his famous "Album for the Young." He tells Reinicke that the first pieces of this were specially written for his eldest child on her birthday, and speaks of the collection as

[1] Wasielewski. The authoress has this incident on the authority of Fräulein Eugenie Schumann, to whom this volume is dedicated.

containing traces of his old humour. He characterises them as "quite distinct from the 'Kinderscenen,' which are recollections of a grown-up person for those of his own age, while the 'Christmas Album' consists more of imaginings, presentiments and future states for younger people."[1] He adds later that he feels that, of all his works, this for the little ones will be the most popular, and he expresses the intention of having an attractive and appropriate cover designed for it, this being subsequently done in most artistic manner by Richter.[2] No father could have been prouder of, or more deeply devoted to, his children than indeed was Schumann; and for his three elder daughters he specially wrote the group of Sonatas known as Op. 118.

[1] Letter to Reinicke, October 6, 1848.
[2] *See* Illustration, p. 183.

CHAPTER XI

Attitude to Professional Friends—Able and Generous Criticism of Fellow-Musicians—Appreciation of, and Affection for, Mendelssohn—An "Affectionate Visit" and Mutual Friendliness—Opinion of Meyerbeer—Wagner and his Music—Kindliness towards Young Students, etc.—Miscellaneous Correspondence—Senses of Detail, Courtesy and Consideration—Pathetically Humorous even to the End—A Significant Letter.

Attitude to Professional Friends

As a friend, it was inevitable that a man in Schumann's foremost position as editor and eminent musician should command a wide and notably distinguished circle. Connected with his staff on the *Neue Zeitschrift* were such eminent critical writers as Zuccalmaglio, whose excellent literary talent he frequently refers to, and with whom he constantly corresponded in terms of the highest appreciation and intimacy. His old master, Dorn, was never forgotten. He addresses him as his "dear and most honoured friend," and makes a confidant of him in many little matters. For Ignace Moscheles Schumann had always, since hearing him play in early childhood, cherished the deepest respect and esteem. Some highly interesting correspondence passed between them which it will repay the reader to look through in the published *Letters.* Shortly after Schumann's "Carnaval" was published, Moscheles had spoken very favourably of it, and this greatly encouraged the young composer. The elder musician criticised some parts of it, but apparently in the kindest spirit. Schumann, in reply, while thoroughly modest in acknowledging his senior's good judgment, defends a little point in the notation with much spirit and effect.[1] In this, as in many other instances wherein Schumann speaks of his own works, albeit with utmost self-restraint, there is always the conscious expression of *savoir-faire* which is inseparable from the true genius which knows because it knows, and gives vent to nothing that it cannot explain. In November 1851 the devotion to the elder master appears as great as ever, for about that time Moscheles accepted the dedication of the fine Sonata for Pianoforte and 'Cello (Op. 121), an honour much appreciated by Schumann, who had been deeply inspired by Moscheles's playing when a little lad.[2]

Able and Generous Criticism of Fellow-Musicians

No trait, indeed, of Schumann's character is so notable and admirable as his respect and modest admiration for the work of fellow-artists and composers. His appreciation of contemporaries was keen and enthusiastic, and his critical estimate of their work of lasting, and in many cases prophetic, value. His early recognition of Chopin, Berlioz, Brahms and others is well known. Musicians are usually accredited with a lack of the nobler feelings of generosity towards each other — that colour-blindness which can allow no rival to the "ego"—but this accusation can certainly not be laid to the charge of

[1] Letter from Leipzig, September 22, 1837. [2] *See* p. 6.

Schumann. He was ever ready to esteem others better than himself, and thus fulfilled at once one of the noblest as well as the most difficult precepts of Christian virtues. We have spoken of the friendly relationship between him and Mendelssohn, and to a certain extent endeavoured to discuss why, seeing the almost ecstatic admiration which Schumann had for his great compeer, Mendelssohn's correspondence is strangely free from reference to the editor-composer. The fact that Schumann, during the period when he was most closely brought into contact with Mendelssohn, was better known as a musical critic than a creative artist, may have somewhat repelled the composer of "St Paul" and "Elijah"—indeed, some discussion as to the legitimacy of art criticism apparently passed between them. Temperamental differences must also be taken into account, as the fact that Mendelssohn's musical ideas—in regard to symmetry, form and polish—were widely at variance with those of his famous contemporary. One little incident of outside testimony may, however, be quoted to disprove the statement that Mendelssohn failed to recognise any merit in the musicianship of Schumann. Christopher Hilf, a noted violinist, reports having overheard Mendelssohn, at a Gewandhaus rehearsal, express a wish to Schumann that he would, in person, conduct his (Schumann's) "beautiful Symphony." But Schumann's reply was: "No, no, it is in the very best hands."[1] Schubring also, in his *Recollections of Felix Mendelssohn Bartholdy*, says that Mendelssohn spoke to him in terms of the highest estimation of Schumann's musicianship, adding that it was not alone for

[1] *Life of Robert Schumann as told in his Letters* (May Herbert).

the sake of Madame Schumann's playing that Mendelssoh fostered a friendship for the Schumanns.

Of one thing we are certain. In Schumann, Mendelssoh had an admirer and champion as sincere as he was devote and enthusiastic. Many letters to different individua contain the most glowing comments upon th gifted "Felix Meritis," as he figured in th mystic Society of the Davidites. Even apa from his esteem for Mendelssohn the compose there existed a real personal affection on th part of Schumann for his brother in musicia ship. While in Dresden, probably just when convalescenc was beginning to cheer him after his long illness of 184 Schumann writes to hope that Mendelssohn still thinks c his friends and asks if they may come to see him often. I the letter [1] Schumann speaks of the severe nervous break down which had so long depressed him and prevented hi from working. He then refers to Clara's playing of the "ol ever-young Caprice in E," [2] which was the first number wit which she tried her new Streicher piano. The write further speaks of having heard accounts of "Œdipus," som organ sonatas, and a new oratorio, and the epistle conclude as follows: "Farewell, my honoured Mendelssohn, an soon send me a line to say whether you still think of your faithfully, Robert Schumann."

Appreciation of Mendelssohn

It is evident, from correspondence that followed, tha Mendelssohn replied in the kindest and most friendl spirit; indeed, he appears to have called upon th Schumanns shortly afterwards, for Schumann writes in th

[1] From Dresden, July 7, 1845. [2] By Mendelssohn.

following September thanking him for his "affectionate visit" and the conversation that then passed between them. Further most interesting correspondence also took place subsequently; and in the October of the year (1845) Madame Schumann played at the Gewandhaus, receiving particularly courteous and kindly treatment from Mendelssohn himself. On the same occasion a repetition performance of Schumann's B flat Symphony was given, which gratified the composer very much. Schumann, writing to express his appreciation of Mendelssohn's geniality towards himself and his wife, speaks of having tried over his (Mendelssohn's) recently published Organ Sonatas on the piano. Nos. 5 and 6 especially appeared to have pleased; and, in most tasteful language, the correspondent contrasts the organ music of Mendelssohn and that of his great predecessor, J. S. Bach. The latter Schumann pictures as sitting at the instrument; the former appears to him as a St Cecilia bending over the keys. "It is really a fact, dear Mendelssohn," says his warm-hearted friend, "that no one else writes such pure harmonies; and they keep on getting purer and more inspired." [1]

An "Affectionate Visit" and Mutual Friendliness

Enough has been said to show that Schumann could fully enter into and take a pride in the attainments of others, and that he was quite free from any spirit of envy or bias whatsoever.[2] He has been accused of not being just to the talents of Meyerbeer, whom he criticises with, for him,

[1] Letter from Dresden, October 22, 1845.

[2] Schumann himself writes: "The artist who refuses to recognise the efforts of his contemporaries may be looked upon as lost."—Letter to Brendel, September 18, 1849.

severity almost approaching disdain. Writing to Hiller he speaks of the music of "Le Prophète" as being "very poor," and that he could not say how distasteful it was to him.[1] It must be remembered that always, in Schumann's estimates of his contemporaries, the aims of the man, as the output of the musician, were taken into account. That Meyerbeer wrote for the populace and for the whim of the moment, rather than in accordance with the higher dictates of classical art, disturbed the righteous mind of the critic whose ideals were ever of the loftiest, and who, if he heartily despised anything, held up the finger of just scorn to all that savoured of time-serving or paltry display.

Opinion of Meyerbeer

With regard to Wagner, Schumann has expressed himself in terms which were undoubtedly prompted by sincerity and critical insight, but they are not altogether flattering to the composer of "Der Ring des Nibelungen." Perhaps his first mention of Wagner in a letter occurs in a communication addressed to Mendelssohn,[2] in which he speaks of Wagner showing the text of his contemplated "Lohengrin" to a group of distinguished art connoisseurs, among whom were Bendemann, Hiller, Reinick (the poet) and Schumann. The text appears to have been admired by all, and the seeing it caused Schumann to abandon thoughts of a plot upon a similar story connected with King Arthur and the Round Table. A couple of months later,[3] Schumann, after hearing "Tannhäuser," thought it striking and original, and much

Wagner and his Music

[1] Letter to Hiller, January 15, 1850.
[2] November 18, 1845.
[3] January, 1846.

superior to Wagner's earlier operas, though some of the music he characterises as "trivial." Yet he adds, almost prophetically, that "he (Wagner) may become of immense importance to the stage,"[1] having the courage and technical knowledge to constitute success. It is curious to note that, nearly seven years later,[2] Schumann is almost scathing about the music of Wagner *apart* from scenic accessories. He calls it "downright amateurish, meaningless and repulsive." He deprecates the artistic taste of the day, which compared German masterpieces of dramatic composition with Wagner's productions, but adds ominously, "The future will decide."[3] Probably Schumann had imbibed a slight personal misunderstanding of his great contemporary.

Kindliness towards Young Students

No feature is so praiseworthy in the disposition of Schumann as his kindly tolerance of, and deep interest taken in, the work of young students and artists. Few men in his exalted and independent position would have taken the trouble to notice beginners in the art of composition who sought his advice, or have set himself the task of answering their letters at length and giving them valuable gratuitous advice. Yet this Schumann did over and over again, never wounding his correspondents with the coldness or rebuke which their temerity doubtless often deserved, but ever entering into their thoughts and aspirations with the devotion of a friend, and, at times, almost of a father, and invariably softening criticisms and corrections of style and

[1] Letter to Dorn, January 7, 1846. [2] In 1853.
[3] Letter to Van Bruyck, May 8, 1853.

workmanship with words of kindly encouragement and most helpful counsel. Young composers, especially for the organ, cannot do better than read that excellent letter of his to the music-teacher, J. G. Herzog of Bruck.[1] Therein Schumann gives proof of his practical knowledge, as of his infinite experience, as a composer. He quaintly warns his correspondent against getting into too easy a way of writing for the organ, as almost anything sounded effective upon it. Not too many things should be written at first, but rather there should be steady practice in the more exalted forms, such as the fugue, of which J. S. Bach had left such notable examples. The applicant is further advised to write for the voice, as being the most helpful aid of all in the development of musicianship, and moreover to sharpen the mental faculties by *reading* as much good music as possible before playing it. He concludes by the comforting injunction to never lose heart, but to confirm courage by turning to the work that the great Germans — Bach, Handel, Mozart and Beethoven — had accomplished. How much Carl Reinicke must have been encouraged, at the commencement of his career, by the beautiful letter of helpful advice and kindly criticism which Schumann wrote him,[2] we can well imagine. In this the composer speaks of the extreme difficulty of being quite original at first, one's early efforts being more or less a reproduction of music already heard. "The ore," he adds, "has to go through a great many washings before it becomes sterling metal."

Almost the last letter, indeed, that this gifted and sym-

[1] Letter to J. G. Herzog, Leipzig, August 4, 1842.
[2] Letter, January 22, 1846.

pathetic scribe penned was to one L. Meinardus, a young musician who had, on more than one occasion, solicited his expert comments and advice upon compositions submitted. Evidently the work done was not up to Schumann's standard of excellence. "I wish," he says, "you composed in the same style as you write your letters—so easy, thoughtful, and full of natural humour."[1] He then proceeds to counsel that beautiful original melody should always be striven for, and that pianoforte music should not have exclusive attention, the study of choral and orchestral writing being specially commended. The writer concludes his note by hoping that all comments will be taken kindly. "I am anxious," he adds, "to help all young and honestly-striving artists, and that is only possible by a frank expression of opinion."

Miscellaneous Correspondence

The marvel was that one so active with his thought and pen on matters of great moment, and one who, really within but a limited period of healthful activity, managed to write such a number of works in such varied forms, found time for the voluminous correspondence which, even as it stands in its present published editions, can but represent a fraction of the letters written. Outside the family, friendly and artistic letters which we have already spoken of come a large number of miscellaneous epistles, many of them of uncommon interest and value as throwing light upon the many-sided mind of this truly marvellous imaginative artist. Thus there are, among others, the beautiful letters to the various correspondents with whom he was in treaty for

[1] Letter, December 28, 1853.

opera and other texts, notably those to the poet Hebbel, for whom he had a profound admiration which was mutually reciprocated. There were also the numerous business letters to publishers—those to the heads of the eminent firm of Breitkopf & Härtel, Leipzig, partaking more of the character of intelligent and friendly intercourse than the transaction of mercantile matters. Nor must it be thought, as is so often alleged, that Schumann wrote invariably in a solemn, if lofty and artistic, strain. In his early letters especially we find frequent traces of playfulness and boyish light-heartedness which developed into a subtle if exalted humour toward the close of his career. An amusing early effusion to his landlady at Leipzig cannot fail to entertain the reader. In it he merrily arranges with her about his lodging, his laundry, and even his diet, giving her a long list of the dishes he likes and dislikes. Of fatty foods, sweets, fruits and jam he is to have none! Soups and broths he particularly favours; he fancies all kinds of fish, eels alone excepted; and so on.[1]

Senses of Detail, Courtesy and Consideration

Like most great inventive minds, Schumann had a keen sense of detail—one might almost call his faculty in this respect a womanly one for minutiæ. We see this coming out in different ways in his private correspondence, no small item of information being considered too trivial for the completion of the word-picture. The composer's consideration for others, and the delicacy and tact with which he transacted even the homeliest duties, were also remarkable. One instance of this may

[1] Letter to Madame Devrient, September 1, 1837.

suffice. During his and Madame Schumann's absence upon the Russian trip of 1844, their children had been left to the care of Carl Schumann, Robert's brother, at Schneeberg. The father and mother called for the young folk on the homeward journey; and later on, upon arrival at their home in Leipzig, the composer wrote a charming letter of acknowledgment and thanks to Herr and Madame Carl Schumann. In this he refers to the expenses and anxieties which the children must have cost their kind guardians. For the latter he can only thank, but for the former he and Clara beg that a certain enclosure—the least amount that the young folk's maintenance must have cost—may be accepted and added to Pauline's pin-money. (Pauline was Carl Schumann's daughter.) "It really will not do for you to be the losers," adds the writer, "while we have been making money." Concluding, he says he feels sure this offer will not be misunderstood or misinterpreted. "If you were in our place you would do just the same, would you not?"[1] How few friends or relatives think of such little matters, and often thoughtlessly mulct those belonging to them on the plea of family connection. Fewer still would have the nice feeling to take the initiative in making a practical return in these cases; and fewest of all would put the matter with such nicety and delicacy. Truly Schumann was, even in the most trivial and ordinary of everyday matters, a man of rare refinement, courtesy and consideration for others—in short, a *gentleman* in every sense of the word.

We have endeavoured to do away with the impression

[1] Letter to Carl Schumann, dated from Leipzig, June 3, 1844.

that Schumann was morose or "impossible" in manner, and have quoted Jansen and others to bear witness to the fact that in early manhood the *maestro* could be light-hearted, merry and genial, and that, in company with others of corresponding enthusiastic temperament, he was as bright and easy a conversationalist as any. His music, despite its undercurrent of poetic melancholy, sparkles frequently with a naïve spirit of hopefulness, jubilance and humorous jollity. Even after the development of that sad mental disorder which overclouded his closing years, Schumann had his bright moments, when the old "jolly" humour would return to him and he could be again as a child among the children. But how strangely do the opposite phases of a sentiment overlap one another, and often merge the one into the other! Thus, under a cloak of aversion, in some reserved and sensitive natures, may we find a devotion too intense for word utterance. Beneath a smiling mask there often hides a tortured heart. The sublime at times verges on ridicule; the odd and humble things of life are seldom apart from the highest nobility of aim and purpose. Pathetic, indeed, in its humour and extravagant phantasy, is almost *the last letter* that Schumann wrote. It was penned to his friend Joachim on February 6, 1854, *exactly three weeks* before the unhappy musician attempted to put a quietus to his over-fervid imaginations in a desperate plunge into the Rhine waters. In this epistle he speaks of having dreamt of being three days with his friend, who appeared to him to have heron's feathers in his hat, from which champagne was running. "How

Pathetically Humorous even to the End

prosaic, but how true!" comments the narrator, probably referring to the sparkle of the great violinist's virtuosity. Then the letter-writer proceeds to tell how he has been working in his Garden,[1] which was growing more and more gorgeous, and that he had been putting up "sign-posts" at various points to prevent folk from going astray—"I mean," he adds, "explanatory notes." History, he says, Homer and Plato all have furnished him with wondrous sayings. Then he refers to music being, for the time, *silent*. It was an ominous remark with a view to the sad earth silence that was soon to fall upon himself as a creative artist. But his friend, in a previous communication, had apparently tried to cheer him up with some choice specimens of his favourite weed. "I like the cigars very much," he says. "There seems to be a Brahmsonian flavour about them which is, as usual, rather strong but tasty. Now I see a smile hovering about him. Now I will conclude: it is getting dark already. Write to me soon—in words and sounds too."[2] And the scribe attached a postscript to say that his wife sent her regards, and he begged also to be remembered to Herr Grimm, who seemed so unlike his name.

This letter is curiously, almost weirdly, symbolic of the man, and *prophetic* of the sad happening that was to follow.

At the time it is clear that, even in sleep, the overwrought imaginative mind could not rest. He saw his friend in

[1] The "Dichtergarten," a collection of musical ideas from the poets, over which Schumann was much occupied at the time.

[2] Last letter quoted in May Herbert's English Translation. It is dated from Dusseldorf, February 6, 1854. On the 27th of the month Schumann attempted to commit suicide.

fantastic garb, yet this he invests with artistic, poetic significance. The love for poetry was as strong with him as ever, just as, when in his teens, he pored over the tomes in his father's book shop and first made the acquaintance of Jean Paul, Byron and Moore. The great models of antiquity in literature and philosophy were as gigantic to him as ever—those titanic minds which he worshipped in early college days. For the time being his music was mute, but in the letter he adds, "outwardly." Fancy this from one who, between his twentieth and fortieth year, had bequeathed such treasures to musical art, and that in every imaginable form—the quantity as the quality of his pianoforte music alone being marvellous! But he still has the solitary thinker's fondness for the philosophic, tranquilising smoke, and, with all that wondrous and sympathetic interest which never left him for young and soaring talent, he saw the face of the coming genius of the youth Brahms, smiling at him through the vaporous curls. But the end was nearing—the end of his letter—the end of his earth work. He speaks of it *getting dark already*. Did the eyes of the seer perceive a greater darkness before him than that of the fading of mortal daylight? May not the shadow of the gloom that already brooded over him, and was fated to find its dispersion only in death, already have been overclouding the mental vision of the poet-musician? Still he can remember his friend, his wife, his acquaintances. He asks Joachim to let him hear speech and *music* soon. And ere he lays down the pen that is soon to forget its cunning, he makes the playful remark of the child—Herr *Grimm* is not like his name!

A Significant Letter

CHAPTER XII

The Man as seen in his Letters—Personal Aspects—Appearance and Build—Taciturnity of Latter Years—A Silent Repast and Interview—Meeting with Wagner—Alleged Vehemence—The Composer's Reserve—Importunacy quietly repressed—The Musician at Home—The Leipzig Music-Room—At the Kaffeebaum—Evening Routine—Schumann's Religion—Opinion of Berlioz, Moscheles and Mendelssohn—Abbé Liszt—*Resumé.*

The Man as seen in his Letters

THUS far the man and his circle, as they came, through his letters to them, within his inner life. The topic is of vast and wonderful interest. If anyone was competent to express an opinion upon the value of our mode of arriving at the personality of this beloved Master-Musician, it was surely Madame Clara Schumann, that faithful and devoted wife, who shared his triumphs as his sorrows, and was by his side through hours of sunshine as through days of gloom. Writing to Fanny Raymond Ritter, when referring to the deficiencies and inaccuracies of the biographies of her husband that had already appeared, Madame Schumann says:—

"I could have wished Schumann to have been placed more truthfully before the public *as a man* (the italics are ours); his works speak sufficiently for him as a musician, while his writings testify to the discrimination of his judgment and the variety of his talents. But the purity of his life, his noble aspirations, the excellence of his heart, can never be fully known, except through the communications of his family and friends, and from his private correspondence."[1]

With such an opinion the most critical cannot but be content; and so it seems almost superfluous to add anything further on the temperamental characteristics of Schumann.

Schumann's Personality

That able Schumann authority, Professor Jansen,[2] describes the composer as of stately and powerful build, adding that, although his clothing was not at all striking or studied, his general bearing was a distinguished one. Truhn, as quoted by Jansen, enters into further particulars. He says that Schumann had a good-sized and very German style of head, which was plentifully covered with fine, dark-fair hair, and a full and beardless countenance, with lips shaped as if in the act of commencing to whistle softly. His eyes, although neither large nor energetic in expression, were of a beautiful blue, and they had an absorbed look about them as if the owner was always intent upon finding out something within his own inner being. He held himself uprightly, but the walk was leisurely—that of one whose bones were loosely put together and hardly compatible with the strong, broad-shouldered figure that he presented. An eyeglass was used a good deal—he was short-sighted—but this without a

[1] Preface to Schumann's *Music and Musicians*, translated from the original German by Fanny Raymond Ritter.

[2] *See* the exhaustive book, *Die Davidsbündler aus Robert Schumann's Sturm und Drange Periode.*

shadow of affectation, as one would well imagine from the honest, straightforward nature of the man himself.

Taciturnity of Latter Years

In personal intercourse he was sparing of words, and this was especially noticeable during the latter part of his career. It might well be said of him, as it had been of Uhland, whom he possibly resembled also in other ways, that he *said* "only half," while others said "the whole," it being remembered that he *felt* the whole, as many feel but the half of what is spoken. His taciturnity was by no means the outcome of surliness or proud indifference. "Few artists," said Hiller, whose personal acquaintance dated from 1839, "were more difficult to describe from their outward bearing than Schumann. His intercourse was entirely opposed to the characteristics of his music. In the latter he expressed himself with all the eloquence of his deeply impressionable soul; in the former his peculiar trait was silence."

Silent Repast and Interview

Brendel gives a remarkable instance of this silence. Schumann had discovered some excellent *Marco-brumer* (wine) at a certain restaurant, and thither he asked Brendel to accompany him to luncheon. During the walk there and back, the only remark Schumann made was about the rare beauty of such a summer day as it happened to be, when all was silence, and perfect peace reigned in Nature. A second excursion of this kind had a similar result. At such times the outward world only existed for Schumann in so much as it chanced to form part of his dreams. He looked upon Society merely as a means to awaken him from the feeling of solitude. This reticence was not so marked in Schumann's early youth and young manhood,[1] but certainly it was aggravated towards his latter years, so much so as to become very trying to strangers or to those who did not fully understand the temperament of the musician. In 1845 Hiller and Concertmeister Schubert took Felicien David to see Schumann. They were received in a friendly way and asked to sit down. "Schubert and I," said Hiller, "kept on talking chiefly in order to break the almost painful silence that had fallen upon us after the first greetings were over. Schumann and David listened to our talk without making any remark, in spite of the opportunities we gave them of doing so. After some time," continued Hiller, "I began to feel oppressed. Presently Schumann said, in a low voice, to me, 'David speaks very little.' 'Not much,' I replied. 'That is nice,' was Schumann's comment as he smiled pleasantly."[2]

Meeting with Wagner

According to Hanslick, Wagner is reported to have said, upon meeting Schumann in 1846, that he was a highly-gifted musician but an impossible being. It appears that when he (Wagner) visited Schumann on his return from Paris he spoke to his fellow-countryman on every possible subject—music, literature, politics, etc.—but all in vain. Schumann remained almost dumb for nearly an hour. "One cannot always speak alone," Wagner is said to have remarked, naturally enough, after narrating the incident. Hanslick further reports that Schumann said of Wagner—referring to this one-sided conversation—that the

[1] *See* page 111 *et seq.*

[2] *Davidsbündler* (Jansen).

composer of "Tannhäuser" was a very well-informed and talented man, but that he talked incessantly and one could not put up with it for long!

Alleged Vehemence

Opposite to this testimony we must place the record of many intimate friends, who have affirmed that Schumann could, at times, be very eloquent, especially in dialogues. This was particularly the case when the talk turned upon artists or compositions in which he was keenly interested. Occasionally he could be even vehement when an opinion was given with which he did not agree, or when remarks were made that hurt his senses of justice and kindliness. Once a celebrated artist, when a guest of Schumann's in 1848, happened to speak in a joking and partially contemptuous manner of Mendelssohn in the composer's presence. For a while Schumann listened in silence. Suddenly, however, he rose, seized his visitor by the shoulder, and exclaimed excitedly, "Sir, who are you to dare to speak so of an artist like Mendelssohn?" With these words Schumann left the room.[1]

Schumann's Reserve

The composer seems to have been himself fully conscious that his silence was often misunderstood and unfavourably commented upon. "Don't think I am sulky," he had said in his quiet, modest way to Madame Voigt, "if I cannot always reply when spoken to." Once, when his friend Zuccalmaglio had announced that he was coming to see him, Schumann answered, "I shall be delighted to see you again, but there is not much to be had from me—I

[1] Jansen.

hardly speak at all—in the evening more, and most at the piano."[1] The fact was that Schumann, as Professor Jansen says, did not belong to that class with whom one could be intimate all at once. "Those who understood his individuality and truthfulness—what he was and what he appeared to be—were devotedly attached to him." The musician's customary reserve in meeting strangers naturally limited his intimate circle. No one than he was more exclusive, in spite of his kindly and amiable ways, in his choice of familiar friends. "He possessed a certain aristocratic manner whereby he invariably succeeded in keeping at a distance people who were inclined to be unsympathetic towards him. Importunate folk and chatterers seldom obtained much access to him, for he understood (the aims of such people) and, with an indescribable grace, quietly dismissed them."[2]

Jansen quotes Truhn as giving an example of this. It seems that a certain Thuringin singer was going round Leipzig with an Easter Cantata which he had composed, endeavouring to find a publisher for it. He succeeded in getting a few kind lines in recommendation of his work from Fink, and, armed with this and the cantata, he forthwith sought out Schumann, in the hope that he too would add a line of introduction or approval. Schumann, upon hearing of Fink's commendation, is reported to have said, "Good, good! Do you not know that the old musical paper (Fink's) is in a state of enmity with the new (the *Neue Zeitschrift*)? I and my fellow-workers are

Importunacy quietly repressed

[1] Jansen. [2] *Ibid.*

considered by the old ones as new as well as devilish romantic, and we have a hard struggle to hold our own. A recommendation from me, the General of the devilish romantic ones, would arouse the suspicion and enmity of Fink, and one from me in my own name would cause your work to remain unpublished for ever. Pin your faith to Fink's introduction and you will soon see the good results." So the musician made his adieux without the recommendation, and Schumann related the occurrence with unusual glee in the evening at the Kaffeebaum. A few days later, when Schumann was taking his customary stroll in the Rosenthal, the singer saluted him and told him, with apparent self-satisfaction, that the work had found a publisher. "There you have the good result," replied Schumann, as, replacing his cigar in his mouth, he continued his way.[1]

Schumann at Home

In his home life Schumann was a pattern of all that was active and methodical. He was a marvellously busy man. Composition, pianoforte playing, writing for the *Neue Zeitschrift*, his large correspondence, as well as reading, of which he was particularly fond, occupied a full day. He never lost his taste for books, and often carried one about with him when out walking, taking every stray chance of looking into it as he went along. His sitting-room was simply furnished, and, when a youth, was as usually topsy-turvy as most students' rooms are. Becker says that, when once in the musician's apartment in 1834, being asked to sit down, he experienced some difficulty in finding a seat, as chairs and sofa were heaped with books and music. In

[1] Jansen in *Die Davidsbündler*.

these early years Schumann often changed his quarters, until, in 1836, he moved into a nicely-situated abode, which he occupied with much comfort and contentment until his marriage in 1840.

Leipzig Music-room

Truhn's description of the workroom of the editor-musician is interesting. "The window looked out upon the most wooded part of the Promenade which surrounded old Leipzig. . . . It was so still in this place that, when the trees rustled in front of the window, one could have fancied oneself placed in a lonely castle surrounded by a wood, as described in the wonderful romances of Eichendorf. . . . In this window nook, and raised from the floor by being placed upon a little platform, was a table on which were to be seen writing materials, an arrangement for hanging a watch, also a charming miniature of a thoughtful-looking girl's head. Schumann's watch, which he wore on a hair chain, was, while he worked, to be found upon the stand. . . . Although this poet's room had only one window in it, there was also space for a grand pianoforte—placed against the opposite wall, through which a door led to the next room—a sofa and a table. . . . The room was oblong in shape. . . . Besides the pictures of Bach, Beethoven, Schunke and his Clara, a Raphael's Madonna also adorned the wall. When Schumann wrote in 1839 from Vienna to announce his return to this apartment, to which he had become attached, he particularly asked that this special picture might not be missing." [1]

In the evenings, after work, it was customary for Schumann

[1] *Die Davidsbündler.*

to frequent Poppe's "Kaffeebaum"—a place of meeting of young men of his own age—where a spirit of good fellowship seems to have reigned, as much apart from onesidedness as it was from bacchanalian excess of any kind. Schumann had a rather retired corner, to which he was particularly partial. Jansen describes him as generally sitting sideways from the table, so that he could lean his head on his hand. Often he would be observed to push back the hair which fell over his forehead. At these times his eyes were half closed and he appeared buried in dreamy musings. "When an interesting exchange of ideas was going on one could see him awakening out of his dreams—I might almost say stepping again into the outer world—and we would then notice the splendour and brightness of his eyes."[1]

At the Kaffeebaum

In this unrestrained society, where, apparently, his silent meditative ways were thoroughly understood and sympathised with, Schumann spent many pleasant hours with the inevitable cigar in his mouth. The drink he usually partook of was beer, but he liked good Rhine wine and champagne. However, in the matter of liquids he was invariably moderate, and frequented the Kaffeebaum more as the man of to-day visits his club of an evening, *i.e.*, in order to have a chat with congenial friends, than in any spirit of conviviality. Often, indeed, he would leave the table suddenly, without bidding good-night to any of the company. In this case he invariably had music in his head, which evidently would

Evening Routine

[1] Jansen.

brook no delay until it was written down at home. Indeed, Schumann's evening visits to the coffee-house were simply a part of his quiet and well-ordered diurnal routine. They formed, doubtless, a pleasant relaxation after the mental exertions of the day, and invariably the charm of his own family circle found him home again at an early hour; for he was never so happy as when in the society of his gifted wife and his children, of whom he was extremely fond.

Schumann's Religion

It is difficult, and would be unbecoming of us, to form an exact opinion upon Schumann's creed. Wasielewski considered him a "Freethinker" in the broadest, most liberal meaning of the word. From intolerance, bigotry or sectarianism the man was decidedly free. In his generous preference of others to himself in the case of gifted contemporaries, he certainly put in practice one of the noblest of Christian maxims. In his kindness to young and unknown musicians he was acting as one who doeth good apart from any desire of return or public applause. A remark, attributed to the composer himself, may give us the most reliable sidelight upon this matter of his Faith. He says: "If a man knows the Bible, Shakespeare and Gœthe, and has taken them into himself, he needs no more." It is not without significance that the devotional form of the Mass attracted him during his last few years of activity.

The opinions upon Schumann—the man and artist—as expressed by some of the most distinguished of his contemporaries and circle, are worthy of note. Schumann's early appreciation of the great gifts of Berlioz is well-known. Berlioz, who was generally most piquant and scathing in his remarks, always cherished a most friendly personal regard for his fellow-worker, and characterises him as "one of the most distinguished composers and critics of Germany." Beyond this remark and Berlioz's warm appreciation of Schumann's "inestimable applause" bestowed upon his own works, it does not appear that the French musician committed himself to a definite estimate of the value of Schumann's work. Wenzel related to Jansen that he had witnessed Berlioz looking through one of Schumann's string quartets, but, although he turned the leaves over very slowly, no remark was forthcoming. The different temperaments of the two men must be remembered, albeit, from many points of view, they held similar lofty and original theories upon their art. To Schumann music was as the food of his soul. Impetuous, fiery Berlioz is reported to have said, "I want music to put me in a fever and shatter my nerves. Do you think I hear music for pleasure?"

Opinion of Berlioz

Moscheles, writing in his diary in 1836, says: "Finger gymnastics find their proper place in Thalberg's new compositions . . . for the intellect give me Schumann. Romanticism strikes me so forcibly in him. His geniality is also so great that I must lose myself more and more in his works in order to estimate fairly the qualities as the weaknesses of the new school." As we have already inferred, there is some difficulty in arriving at the exact opinion which, as a musician, Mendelssohn held of Schumann. The personal friendship between the two great contemporaries is an assured fact. We regret that the

Moscheles and Mendelssohn, etc.

composer of "St Paul" (of which work Schumann so frequently speaks with the most intense enthusiasm) leaves us no opinion either upon his friend's individuality or his work as a musician, the little remark, quoted upon hearsay in page 129, as to Schumann's "beautiful" Symphony, being all we have been able to discover. Here, again, the diverse natures of the two men must account for much. Mendelssohn's charming, almost "sugary," personality is seen in his clear melody and polished harmonies; Schumann's mute soul-yearnings only dawn upon us after a long and loving analysis of his often veiled, if richly-coloured, tone poems. In the same way the philosophic and determined Wagner failed to "draw out" the sensitive dreamer. Schubert, had he lived, and Chopin, had he seen more of him, might have experienced all the charms of the highest type of artistic soul communion—that which wants not words to emphasise it—with our hero.

Characterisation by the Abbé Liszt

Of all the distinguished galaxy of musicians with whom Schumann came in contact, few so intuitively and justly estimated his characteristic traits as Liszt. "He" (Schumann), says the famous Abbé, "appears to us good and lovable, as is every sublime personality; gifted and variable like every true artist; with a predilection for digressions and surprises which denote the poet; before and above all, however, as a straightforward man in his convictions and the manner in which he expresses them. His criticisms present a fine example of a somewhat strict, but really kindly-intentioned, mind, which, while expecting a great deal for art, is indulgent towards artists; who, from his home in the clouds, is pleased to visit, in a friendly manner, those on a lower plane; who pardons much to those of high aspirations; who encourages honest opinions and persevering efforts; who protests with courage and indignation against gifted intelligences who will not use their talents solely for art; who, even in blame, is merciful to the weak, and in praise is never cringing to the successful—being honourable to all." [1]

To add aught to such a kindly and able characterisation by a great pianist-composer of a brother artist seems superfluous; so, with Liszt's words, we take leave of this part of our work. Therein the writer has endeavoured to allow Schumann to present himself, through his circle, in his aspects as son, lover, husband, father, friend—and in all of these capacities he calls for our deepest respect and admiration. If he was over-tainted with romanticism, it formed part of the hypersensitiveness of a peculiarly refined and gentle nature. If we discover him morbid and even superstitious at times, much of this is to be attributed to that poet's nature of his which always hankered after the mysterious and the unseen. In his wondrous freedom from envy or petty narrowness we see the true nobility of his disposition. From the fact that he was both *littérateur* and musician we perceive an explanation of his many-sidedness and liberality of thought. That, spite of his alleged reticence and reserve, he attracted around him a *coterie* of devoted friends and admirers, who included some of the foremost poets and musicians of the day, gives us an insight to the rare personal qualities of the man himself who, with-

[1] *Die Davidsbündler.*

out effort, and as it were insensibly, drew within his magic circle the truest and best essence of the artistic life of his country. Essentially Teutonic in earnestness and uprightness of aim and endeavour, when matched with Bach, Mozart, Schubert, Beethoven and Wagner, Schumann, although partaking of the traits of these great musical minds, stands forth a unique figure upon a pedestal of his own making. Thus in him we see a Master-Musician without model and without disciple, save as far as his originality of tone colouring and grouping, as his intensity of underlying expression, opened up new and undreamt-of fields of thought for generations of so-called "romantic" composers yet to come. From the narrative of his life we may gather the environments which influenced him and the circumstances under which he waged the imaginary war of the Davidsbündler. As he dealt with and appeared to his circle we can understand the kind of man that he was. In his literary and musical output we can best judge of the force of his genius.

Schumann: The Musician and Writer

CHAPTER XIII

Pianoforte Playing—Manner of Performance—Dörffel's Testimony—Improvising at Twilight—Other Authorities.

Pianoforte Playing

WITH regard to Schumann's pianoforte playing, Jansen has gathered a few records which remind one not a little of the executive gifts of Chopin, allowing for the fact that accident had impaired the hand of the subject of our biography. Töpken speaks of Schumann's playing of some of his earlier compositions, especially the "Toccata," which he took at *allegro commodo* speed, and therefore not at the rate to which we are accustomed. In duet and four-handed performances Schumann always took the treble, and Töpken describes him as finding particular pleasure in the rendering, in this way, of Schubert's Polonaises, which he played with much expression. Frequent improvisations are also mentioned. "I own," says Töpken, "that these spontaneous musical effusions of Schumann have always afforded me an enjoyment that, later on, no matter what famous artists I have heard, I never experienced. Ideas poured in upon him in abundance, and were never exhausted. From one principal thought all else seemed to spring forth without effort, and, throughout all, his peculiar genius, with all its depth and originality, as with its magic of poetry, strongly attracted the listener."[1]

It seems that Schumann best liked to play at the twilight hour, and appears to have been happiest over his performance when quite alone, as might be expected from one of his reserved and dreamy nature. At the same time he was always ready to play to his friends. Lorenz says, "His performance was, above all, original, and the exact opposite of that of *virtuosi*, who make imposing effects by strength of percussion and sharp contrasts." Upon the authority of Lorenz we also learn that Schumann seldom played single complete pieces, but rather short, fanciful effusions in preference to anything published or written down. His style of playing, the narrator considered, resembled what one might expect from the nature of the Eusebius numbers in the *Davidsbündler*. His almost uninterrupted, but ever discreet, use of the pedal is also referred to, Lorenz adding that nevertheless no discordant mingling of harmonies was heard,

Manner of Performance

Alfred Dörffel, who was introduced to Schumann in 1839, and who frequently played the composer's own compositions before him, speaks with kindliest recollection of much useful advice from Schumann himself as to the way in which he wished his works rendered. "It is all too stiff," Schumann once commented, when the young performer had been interpreting some of the earlier works, such as "Fantasiestücke" and the "Novelletten." "This remark,"

Dörffel's Testimony

[1] *Die Davidsbündler.*

says Dörffel, "was of great use to me, as it enabled me afterwards to attain a far freer and easier touch."[1] The pianist also speaks of the invariable friendliness of Schumann towards him. "He" (Schumann) "had so much of the mildness of a father that I was not only extremely fond of him, but also always approached him with confidence, whereas I often went tremblingly to Mendelssohn, and, through my nervousness before him, seldom played as well as I otherwise could have done."[2] Dörffel further describes what he calls Schumann's "organ style" of pianoforte playing, and confirms the remark of Lorenz in regard to the composer's fondness for the pedal. It seems that Schumann always kept the pedal somewhat open, so that there was ever a slight mingling of the middle harmonies, and that he was also very adroit at "springs," *i.e.*, in striking one low note alone or in octave, and from thence rapidly and smoothly springing to a chord higher up on the keyboard.

Improvising at Twilight

The following description of Schumann's playing "at the twilight hour," quoted by Professor Jansen in *Die Davidsbündler*, on the authority of this same Alfred Dörffel, reminds one forcibly of the tales that are told of J. S. Bach's improvisations to the shadows in the Thomas Kirche. It appears that Schumann had a pedal keyboard attached to his grand piano. Dörffel expressed a desire to hear him play, and was told to come when the dusk was falling. The young man came accordingly, and, hearing the composer playing within, knocked once or twice at the

[1] Jansen. [2] *Ibid.*

door but received no answer. "Quietly opening the door," says Dörffel, "I therefore entered the room and placed myself silently near the entrance. It was already so dark that Schumann could not see me. He continued to improvise while I listened breathlessly. In the course of about ten minutes he wanted to light his cigar, and by ts gleam he perceived me." Schumann smoked very strong Havanna cigars, it seems, and Dörffel mentions parenthetically that there were many remains of them upon his desk. At first the composer was somewhat surprised to see the mute listener; but, upon matters being explained, he smiled and said it was all right. "What he had been improvising," continues Dörffel, "made a great impression upon me, and I recognised it afterwards in one of the 'Nachtstücke' (which I cannot now remember). The playing moved me in a strange manner. It seemed as if the pedals were always half down, so that the note groups mingled; the melody, however, stood out softly, like the twilight. He (Schumann) must have had exceptional execution (or agility) as a player."[1]

Other Authorities

Truhn, who had heard Schumann play from the "Kinderscenen," "Novelletten" and "Kreisleriana," writes:—"Schumann's playing was indescribable. He moved his fingers with almost alarming rapidity, as if ants were groping about the keys. He played his own compositions (others' works I certainly never heard him perform) with very slight accent but considerable use of both pedals. Yet in this habit of his there was not the slightest want of taste." Brendel

[1] From *Die Davidsbündler*.

expresses himself in the same way about Schumann's peculiarities as a performer, and speaks of it as giving him an insight into the character of the composer's works at that period. Knorr, who must frequently have heard him play as a young man, years afterwards spoke with intense admiration of Schumann's improvisations, and characterised, in particular, a certain "dying away" (vanishing) mode of *diminuendo* which he favoured, "which fell softly upon the ear and won the heart." Even the somewhat phlegmatic F. Whistling seems to have been strangely affected upon once hearing Schumann try a grand piano. This performance he described as essentially original, and so striking that, as long as he lived, he would never forget it. Hauptmann and Spohr also refer in enthusiastic terms to the rare and apparently unique charm of Schumann's playing. Spohr had visited him and heard him perform when passing through Leipzig in 1838, and he speaks, in his *Autobiography*, of being delighted with the composer's rendering of several of his interesting "Fantasiestücke" (Op. 12).

CHAPTER XIV

A Liberal Education—Regarding Talent and Genius—The Inexpressible Ego—Music and Metaphor—Essays from the *Neue Zeitschrift*—Adverse Comments—Defence of the Editor-Musician—Literary *versus* Musical Work.

SCHUMANN, as author and composer, presents an almost unique figure in the history of Master-musicianship. It is true that Berlioz and Wagner, as librettists and journalists, have left records of their critical and literary skill behind them. Again, Weber, Mendelssohn and others were expert at penmanship, and, in their correspondence especially, have shown themselves facile in letter as in "note" writing. There is, however, in most musical authorship which one meets with, a certain onesidedness —a tendency to clothe one's language in technicalities not appreciable to the general public—in fact, a kind of "shop talk" (if we may transpose an apt colloquial expression)—which, though interesting to the initiated, scarcely appeals outside a charmed circle, and leaves the casual reader little wiser than he was before. In the musical scribe this is almost inevitable. His education, from early youth up, has taught him to think in the phraseology of Notation. His surroundings are usually those of the art. His occupations range from the theoretical to the practical work of his profession. His leisure moments are most often spent listening to the musicianship or the musical opinions of others. If he reads at all—and there are some who say "the musician never reads books"!—it is in a kind of desultory way. His hobbies outside his calling are naturally of rather a recreative than a studious kind. Even if he travels, the music of other nations interests him more than their ethnology, religion or politics. The artist cannot help himself. It is part of his disposition to live in an atmosphere of tone forms.

Liberal Education

With Schumann things were different. Although his musical genius early displayed itself, he did not grow up in musical environments. His father's tastes were literary; his mother, though keenly sympathetic, emotional and cultured, could scarcely be called musical. From his childhood Robert saw life from other aspects than that of the onesidedness of music. In his youth, poetry and literature (classic and modern) had a large share of his affections. Well on into his early manhood, his university legal studies (such as they were) and his *penchant* for philosophy kept him from getting into a groove. Hence we find him a man of many parts, and one who was ever striving to shake himself free from near-sightedness of mental vision and narrowness of scope. Thus, while he wrote pre-eminently of music and musicians, and for a music-loving public, there is a certain generality and picturesqueness about his literary work that makes it readable for its style, piquancy and originality, and charms us from its rich strength and beauty of imagery, quite apart from the subject-matter of which it treats.

Regarding Talent and Genius

The fact was that Schumann, like most many-sided intellects, was a close (and kindly) observer of human nature. We see this in almost everything he wrote, and especially in his aphorisms, which might well be characterised, like Shakespeare's sayings, as "household words." Take, for instance, his views upon the difference between Talent and Genius. "Talent," he says, "labours, genius creates."[1] Following out the idea in its detail, we also find that Schumann scarcely agreed with the well-known saw that genius consists in "the capacity for taking infinite pains." This, anyway, is not what genius itself feels when it is in activity. "It is the case of talent," writes Schumann, "that, although it labours more steadily and perseveringly than genius, it does not reach a goal; while genius, floating on the summit of the ideal, gazes above, serenely smiling."[2] In expressions such as these there is no limitation to the world of music only. In art, literature, even mechanism, we form our own private corollaries from the proposition, and feel such utterances as universal truths. That Schumann was the originator of these maxims, those who are familiar with the great schools of philosophic writings will scarcely allow. There is no copyright in fact. But genius knows best how to bring it—and the burning truths of existence—home to many hearts. Thus it is possible that

[1] Schumann's *Music and Musicians* (English Translation by Fanny Raymond Ritter).

[2] *Ibid.*

we all realise the value of using opportunity, of striking the iron while it is hot, of taking time by the forelock, and so on. Schumann thus crystallises the idea when he characterises the secret of success to consist in "understanding of the passing moment while it passes."[1]

A few of Schumann's proverbs have the additional charm of directing our thoughts to that most interesting of problems—the complexity of one's own soul. Take what he says about an ideal. "It is more difficult for a man to discover his own ideal within his own heart than in that of another."[2] It is probable that not a few of us, in self-egotism, will deny this. We think we know ourselves; but do we? Who does? Else were we all giants and geniuses, thoroughly self-reliant, independent and totally free from obligation to our neighbours. The trouble is that we are ever forging fetters of our own making and incarcerating ourselves in self-made prisons. "He who sets limits to himself will always be expected to remain within them,"[3] says Eusebius, *alias* Robert Schumann.

The Inexpressible Ego

Nor, even when he treats of music and musical matters, does Schumann forget the great outside public who know not the jargon of the calling but can enjoy a neatly-put metaphor, no matter of what subject it treats. Schumann compares Music to Chess. Melody is the Queen; Harmony the King. How keenly those who know the moves of the Royal game will relish reading that "The Queen has the most power, but the King turns the scale."[4] Even in com-

Music and Metaphor

[1] *Music and Musicians.* [2] *Ibid.* [3] *Ibid.* [4] *Ibid.*

paring such two poles in the profession as Rossini (of operatic fame) and Beethoven (of sonata and symphony celebrity), our author-musician has something readily attractive to say. Concerning the coming in contact of the two, "Eusebius" writes: "The butterfly flew in the way of the eagle; he moved aside lest he might have crushed the insect with the beating of his wings." There is sarcasm in this, but it is scarcely bitter and certainly not malignant. The butterfly is a thing of beauty, and we feel sad to think of its ephemeral existence. The eagle soars aloft and lives alone in the mountain fastnesses. He is a terror to many; a glory only to those of his own calibre who can afford to set conventionality at defiance. That Schumann was a hero-worshipper in his own department of art, it is not difficult to perceive. With the addition of his predecessor, Schubert, he acknowledged three great master-musicians of surpassing genius. "So that genius exists," he says, "it matters little how it appears; whether in the depths, as with *Bach;* on the heights, as with *Mozart;* or in the depths and the heights at once, as with *Beethoven.*"[1] A more vivid or succinct comparison of these three great composers has perhaps never before been made. Schumann, as a writer, had the rare art of thus placing in a nutshell, or depicting in a miniature, the attributes of others. He even utilises this gift in his music. Witness the panorama of personalities who are introduced in his "Carnaval."

Schumann's Collection of Essays, known by its English (translated) title as *Music and Musicians*, was a reprint, in its original (German) issue, under his own editorship, of

[1] *Music and Musicians.*

papers and essays that had appeared from time to time during the years when he was actively at the head of the *Neue Zeitschrift*. There is no need here to say more of the "Davidsbündler" Society, that mystic musical circle which really only existed in the mind of its originator. The poetry, as the philosophy, of the idea is at once apparent. The skill with which Schumann worked in his art ideas, under the various phases of mild, ecstatic and moderate criticism, beneath the names of Eusebius, Florestan and Master Raro respectively, is worthy of the highest praise.

Essays from the Neue Zeitschrift

Many have been the adverse and wholly unjust comments with regard to Schumann as a literary man and editor. Perhaps the most uncalled-for of all was embodied in a remark of Lobe's to the effect that the composer's great fame was attained unworthily, not by the inherent strength of his creative work, but "through the pens and journal of a shameless *coterie*."[1] Jansen takes up the cudgels victoriously for him in this matter and brings evidence to prove that, up to the end of Schumann's period of presidency over the *Neue Zeitschrift*, in July 1844, out of the forty-six or so of the editor's musical works that had hitherto been published, only *five*[2] had been named in the paper, and these merely by way of mention as having appeared. As Schumann himself wrote to Keferstein, any attempt by an artist to influence public opinion concerning personal works

Adverse Comments

[1] *Musikalishe Briefe eines Wohlbekannten* (Lobe).
[2] Op. 10 (1836), Op. 2, 4 and 5 (1835) and B flat Symphony (1843).

done was hateful to him. "To-day," says Jansen, "we know the man and artist Schumann well enough to laugh at these criticisms" (*i.e.*, the adverse comments).

Defence of the Editor-Musician

The editor-musician himself puts the whole matter honestly and clearly enough in a letter to Kossmaly, written in the spring of 1843. Even as late as this year, the one preceding the last of his connection with the *Neue Zeitschrift*, Schumann speaks of his own compositions as being yet but little known, quoting as reasons the fact, acknowledged by himself, that they were not readily easy of comprehension in construction and material; that he himself, not being an executive artist, was unable to render them in public; and that, being editor, he was debarred from referring to them in his own paper; and that Fink, being the editor of the other paper, could scarcely mention them.[1] That Schumann used his press influence *for others*, to the almost utter exclusion of self, is evident to any careful reader of his essays. But the man was far from being insensible to criticism. He seems to have highly valued the opinions of his erudite contemporaries, and, indeed, to have keenly suffered from adverse notice or comment of any kind. At one time he approached Dorn, hoping he would give him a place in his Gallery as the world knew so little of him; saying playfully that, in the main, he agreed with Jean Paul that "air and praise are the only things man can and must always swallow."[2] Upon the approach of his marriage, too, he seems to

[1] Letter to Kossmaly, May 5, 1843.
[2] Letter to H. Dorn, September 5, 1839.

have been naturally anxious that the press should take some recognition of him and his distinguished wife that was to be, and so expresses himself to that effect in the letter to Keferstein just referred to.[1] Therein he confessed to be too proud to influence Fink through his friends the Härtels, and strongly depreciated any courting of public criticism by the artist himself. But, for his beloved Clara's sake, it is evident that such encouragement would please him as it would cheer her. In the letter already mentioned as written later to Kossmaly (in 1843), he concludes by remarking that although formerly he did not care whether people noticed him or not, matters were different since he had a wife and family to consider. Surely these side-lights upon the straightforwardness and integrity of the man entirely free him from the calumny of ever being guilty of "blowing his own horn."

Literary versus *Musical Work*

Another matter of debate in connection with Schumann's literary labours was that these militated against his musical output, and prevented him giving that thorough devotion to composition which the exigencies of so all-engrossing an art demanded. It is worthy of note that this criticism comes mainly from the musical fraternity proper, which is not, as a rule, inclined to many-sidedness in art. While it is absolutely true that the shoemaker should stick to his last, the mere paltriness of ostracising a man from the highest achievement because he looks not at life through one pair of spectacles alone, is too palpable to need comment. There can be but one ruling passion in the soul of

[1] Page 165.

a man, but it may find its outlet in varied ways, and the more varied the wider his world of influence. Schumann puts the matter fairly when he mentions [1] that his editing the paper was but a secondary consideration to him, much as he enjoyed the work. "For," he adds, "it is the duty of every man to develop the higher gifts which are given him." Later on, in the same connection, Schumann says that any reproach upon his editorial duties is scarcely warranted, as he worked so hard at "other things" as being part of that "higher destiny" which he felt called upon to fulfil in his life. In fact, as he says,[2] literature, personal environment, as also his own individual experiences, all influenced him; and through these he intimates that he began to compose from his earliest years, soon getting to an understanding of Beethoven and Bach. Far from fettering his musicianship then, the authorship of Schumann was one of the many channels through which his poetic wealth of imagery found an outlet. The mere musician, who is only such, never rises to a real appreciation of his art or his own powers. Had Wagner not been endowed with a fervid perception of the philosophic meaning of the Nibelungen sagas, and had not had the ability to put his thoughts into tangible shape, the famous "Ring" would probably never have come into existence.

[1] Letter to his friend Keferstein.
[2] Letter to Edward Krüger, June 1, 1839.

CHAPTER XV

Forging Ahead with "Full Steam" on—The Musician as Critic—Sensitiveness to Criticism—Style as a Writer—Some Remarkable Essays—Mendelssohn *versus* Meyerbeer—Interesting Miscellaneous Topics—Valuable Musical Advice and Opinions—The Writer as Poet.

Forging Ahead with "Full Steam" on

ALTHOUGH Schumann himself, during his editorship, occasionally expressed the longing to relinquish writing and devote himself entirely to music,[1] yet it is significant that some of the best and freshest of his works were composed during the years 1835 to 1844—his period of full responsibility in connection with the *Neue Zeitschrift*. That the musical world lost little from him through his devotion to penmanship may then be accepted without much demur. There are some natures which work best when forging ahead with "full steam" on. To these a single aim or impetus is scarcely sufficient for fervid endeavour; added energies come to cope with extra work, and there is a certain triumph about leaving no detail undone in a many-sided avocation which does not come into the measured fulfilment of a monotonous line of action. Thus Schumann the writer may be said to have strengthened

[1] Letter to Dorn, his "dearest master and friend," April 24, 1839.

the hands of Schumann the musician, though not certainly through advertising his own wares. It was in this respect that even Mendelssohn perhaps slightly misunderstood his great contemporary.[1]

Schumann as Critic

In regard to Schumann's abilities as a critical writer we have already given testimony in quoting his ever-charitable, though thoroughly just and unbiassed, as often marvellously striking and prophetic, verdict upon the work of other musicians and artists. His reverence for the older masters, and especially Bach, is well-known. Some of his sayings about the great Cantor of the Thomas Schule, Leipzig, have become musical aphorisms, such as the making Bach one's "daily bread," etc. That Schumann practised what he thus preached to young students is evident. He speaks of Bach as like his Bible—"day by day." He further refers to Mozart and Haydn having had but an imperfect perception of Bach through want of familiarity with his works. He considered that all "the thoughtful combinations, the poetry and the humour of modern music originated chiefly in Bach."[2] His contemporaries of the so-called German romantic school—among whom he mentions Mendelssohn, Bennett, Chopin and Hiller—he instances as approaching nearer Bach in their compositions than did Mozart. "I myself," he concludes by saying, "confess my sins daily to that mighty one, and endeavour to purify and strengthen myself through him."[3] When he characterises Bach as "unfathomable" we think of Coleridge's estimate of Shakespeare—"myriad-minded indeed he was." Doubtless Bach is to our fore-

[1] *See* page 27, [2] Letter to Keferstein, January 31, 1840. [3] *Ibid.*

most musical spirits what the Bard of Avon is to the *littérateur*—the great rock upon which rests the glorious reputation of the language.

Sensitiveness to Criticism

He who could thus enter into the creative output of others, and so fervently and fondly give to each a worthy laurel crown of appreciation, was himself painfully sensitive to, and hurt by, criticism which displayed the spirit of superficiality or want of thorough understanding of the subject-matter. Schumann knows how to defend himself—in fact, no one was able to do so better—and this he does in a manly and conscientious way. When a certain critic [1] wrote of the "Kinderscenen" that the music was "awkward" and "narrow-minded," he criticises the critic. The discriminator had erred in his judgment. It was not "a screaming child" he (the composer) had got his ideas from. Though child faces had been before his mental vision when composing, the titles of the pieces had been an after-consideration, and had simply been intended as mildly suggestive of the conception as the interpretation of the music.[2] Concerning anyone who, in sheer ignorance, constituted himself an adviser or judge, Schumann could be severely scathing. To a certain young man who had written offering him a text for an opera, and at the same time had remonstrated with the musician to give up romanticism and write music that people could understand, Schumann indited an epistle which must have made the luckless recipient think twice in future before he expressed an

[1] Rellstab.

[2] Letter to H. Dorn, Leipzig, September 5, 1839.

opinion upon matters out of his depth.[1] We have also said that, after Dr Krüger's verdict upon the opera, "Genoveva," the composer wrote so strong a letter to the critic that the intimacy between the two friends terminated. To describe this warm championship of his own output as egotistical on the part of Schumann, is unjust. No man was really more modest than he. But it was the diffidence of genius. When he uttered what was within him he only did so in the firm belief that he had something which was worth the saying. To recant would have been treason to his better intelligence and to the motives that inspired him. What he had written he had written, and he was prepared to stand by it without flinching.

Style as a Writer

Schumann's style as a writer is that of a cultured thinker who has something worth saying and knows how to say it clearly, succinctly, and in such a manner as to appeal, with pleasing imagery, to a wide and varied circle of readers. His epigrams, having the air of spontaneity about them, never appear studied or overweighted—he says enough, and no more, to imprint a vivid mental image of a definite thought-germ from which other intelligences may develop a whole series of resultant ideas. His criticisms, being couched in such an original way, stir us as no mere cut-and-dry description of a man or his works could do. Thus, one who knows not a note of music might take up the article on Hector Berlioz and his Symphonic Poem, "An Episode in the Life of an Artist" (Op. 4), and read it with intense pleasure, apart entirely from any technicalities that are

[1] See *Letters* (English Translation, Vol. II., page 146).

mentioned therein. This is true art; and had Schumann not had a literary as well as a musical training, he could not thus have learnt how to write for the general public. So we would again emphasise that the many-sidedness of Schumann's education comes out best in his penmanship (literary), and as a critical writer of eminence he must always occupy a worthy place in German literature.

Some Remarkable Essays

The exact nature of Schumann's literary work may best be described by referring briefly to one or two of his most famous short articles. The first in the published series (as collected and arranged by himself),[1] known as "An Opus 2," is a fair specimen. In this he treats, in the most vivid, descriptive style, of Chopin's early Variations upon Mozart's celebrated duet from "Don Giovanni," "La cì darem la Mano." Enthusiasm, emotion—indeed rapture—characterise the opinions of "Eusebius" and "Florestan"; even "Master Raro's" maturer judgment implies an interest to see the new composition. "I bend," says the writer, "before Chopin's spontaneous genius, his lofty aims, his mastership."[2] This was the first public (press) recognition of the great Polish composer, and it probably had no little share in making Chopin's name known to musical Leipzig and its surroundings. Occasionally Schumann speaks as if he were an orator whose province it was to stir his listeners by an eloquent appeal to their senses of duty and right. When pleading for a monument to Beethoven, no public speaker could more

[1] *Gesammelte Schriften über Musik und Musiker*, Leipzig, 1854. (English Translation, *Music and Musicians*," by F. R. Ritter.)

[2] *Ibid.*

powerfully thrill an audience than would the following words rouse the earnest, musical-minded German:—"Rise, throw off your indifference, and remember that his monument will also commemorate yourselves!"

Schumann's critical comments upon noted contemporaries, as tributes paid to great predecessors like Bach, Mozart, etc., are among the most valuable portions of his writings. In this connection readers are specially recommended to read his opinions upon Sterndale Bennett, Field, Gade, Henselt, Heller, Hiller, Liszt and many others. With regard to Mendelssohn, this generous brother composer was always the most enthused of champions. The following, among many other remarkable excerpts, may serve to show how keen and how kindly was the estimate at which Schumann valued the output of his fellow-worker:—"It sometimes seems," he says, "as though this artist (Mendelssohn), to whom accident gave the right name[1] at his baptism, broke off a few measures and chords from his "Midsummer Night's Dream," and enlarged and evolved them into separate works, as painters have repeated their Madonnas in angels' heads."[2]

Mendelssohn versus Meyerbeer

A notable essay also is that in which Schumann compares the respective successes of his favourite Mendelssohn and the well-known object of his aversion, Meyerbeer. The editor-musician has been censured as having been unduly severe in this article upon "Les Huguenots" and its composer. Certain it is that seldom has a famous work got

[1] Felix, *i.e.*, "the happy one."

[2] Upon the "Three Caprices" (Op. 33) of Mendelssohn, from *Music and Musicians*.

so thorough a slating from an expert pen. In "Il Crociato," says the critic, he was inclined to place Meyerbeer among musicians; in "Robert le Diable" he began to doubt whether he had not made a mistake in so doing; in "Les Huguenots" the music was best fitted for circus people! Could anything be more scathing? Yet we must remember that Schumann ever went by motive rather than achievement. That Meyerbeer could write Italian, German and French operas, according as the fashion of the moment demanded one or other variety from his facile pen, was enough for this high-souled son of the Fatherland, who strenuously despised work for gain or fame if he considered art was relegated to a secondary place. Several there are who will commend Schumann for taking this stand. But, after all, if the musician be looked upon *par excellence* as a public entertainer, is it altogether a fair view of the case? Music is made to be listened to. The wider the circle of listeners, the greater the beneficent or pleasurable influence. As long as the means used to enthral the public are worthy and legitimate, are we authorised to cavil thereat? Schumann animadverts upon the plot of Meyerbeer's masterpiece. On the same grounds few opera *libretti* are entirely blameless. It cannot be said, for instance, that Mozart's "Don Giovanni" is precisely the kind of tale our young folk are benefited by reading. Yet we must pause ere we condemn. The stage is supposed to hold the mirror up to nature. If vice is punished and virtue rewarded or transferred to a worthier sphere, we may surely always draw a helpful moral lesson from the narration. The courage and religious fervour of the fearless French Protestants are, however, worthier themes than the follies of a Spanish libertine. Perhaps if Meyerbeer had been poor and struggling, as was Mozart, Schumann would not have been so severe upon him.

In the article referred to, Schumann contrasts Mendelssohn's oratorio "St Paul," performed at the same time in Leipzig as "Les Huguenots," with the French opera named, speaking of the sacred work as "of pure art, the creation of peace and love." Very valuable also are his remarks as to the title of the composition. It is spoken of as a "concert oratorio," even as a "Protestant concert oratorio." Later on, in a criticism of Löwe's "John Huss," he qualifies that work as a "sacred opera" and a "dramatic oratorio." Evidently he felt the want of adequate terms to describe the *dramma per musica* when it deals with religious or solemn topics. It is curious, in this connection, to note that Schumann's own "Paradise and the Peri" has been called a "profane oratorio."

Interesting Miscellaneous Topics

Among miscellaneous types of Schumann authorship we might instance his "Characteristics of the Keys." In this most musicians will agree with the remark that, though much may be said on both sides, the truth lies more in the middle. Schumann's fanciful characterisation of the Major mode as the masculine (active), and the Minor as the feminine (passive or suffering) principle, seems apt, and recalls to us his comparison of the Queen (Melody) and the King (Harmony) in the game of chess.[1] Pleasing, and very widely readable also, is his method

[1] Page 163.

of treating *The Literature of Dancing*, in which some productions of the time by Kessler, Thalberg, Clara Wieck, Schubert, etc., are airily and prettily diagnosed by his capable pen. From a purely erudite point of view, most valuable of all Schumann's writings are, perhaps, his critical articles on specific art forms as demonstrated in the work of the composers of his time. In the course of these essays we get an authoritative musical verdict upon many famous works which the world has since fully sanctioned. Therein also are crystallised the names and works of many whose fame was but local and ephemeral save for these references. We commend our readers to a perusal of these in the second series of *Music and Musicians*.[1]

Valuable Musical Advice and Opinions

Schumann's opinions on many matters, as embodied in his writings, are also of the highest worth and utility. His advice and "Maxims," addressed to young musicians, deserve the earnest attention of all music students. If these could be summarised very briefly we might state that they embody exhortations to play scales advisedly, to cultivate habits of accurate time keeping, to see that one's piano is always in tune, and to form the habit of hearing music in one's mind as much as possible.[2] Upon debatable matters, the opinions of a thinker and musician of Schumann's calibre must always carry weight. The legitimacy of "arrangements" has often been called into account. Schumann has something inter-

[1] Fanny Raymond Ritter's English Translation.

[2] Elsewhere Schumann speaks poetically of "the veiled enjoyment of music one does not hear" (on "An Opus 2").

esting to tell us with regard to Liszt's brilliant transcriptions of some of Schubert's songs. These (Liszt's transcriptions) he speaks of as having been stigmatised as the most difficult things ever written for the pianoforte, and he jokingly refers to the remark of some amateur as to whether an *easier* "arrangement" would not restore the *Lied* to its original form again. Then, most convincingly, he debates the "right" to arrange. "A bungler," he remarks, "is ridiculous when he does it badly, but we approve of the intelligent artist's arrangement unless he destroys the sense of the original." [1]

The Writer as Poet

Before leaving the subject of Schumann's authorship, a word might be said as to his poetic inclinations. During his youth, and especially in the course of that nine years when the spell of Jean Paul, Byron and others was upon him, he wrote verses which display an ingenuity of imagination and a flow of rhythm that might well justify one in saying that, had *Music* not had a stronger claim upon him, he could have won a niche in the "Poets' Corner" of his country. While it is true that some celebrated poets appear to have been wholly wanting in an appreciation of music, the keen ears of musicians are seldom indifferent to the measured beat of well-constructed verse or the melody of vocal and flowing syllables. Occasionally they can even find a poetry in prose, as undoubtedly is the case in the oratorio settings of Scriptural texts by Handel, Mendelssohn and others. The natural romanticism of Schumann inclined him to poetry—

[1] On "Liszt's Transcription of some Schubert Songs" (*Music and Musicians*).

the language of the dreamer and the idealist. He was particularly fastidious also in his choice of words for setting to music; witness the long and unfortunately fruitless correspondence with Pohl about a word-book for "Luther."[1] In the matter of a libretto for "Genoveva" it is to be remembered that, failing to get adequate aid from Reinick and Hebbel (the author of the drama), Schumann himself turned librettist and produced a text, if not practically adapted to the best stage requirements, at least an indisputable piece of artistic workmanship from a poetical point of view.

[1] Page 82, *et seq.*

CHAPTER XVI

Piano Compositions—Music for Young People—Pianoforte Sonatas—Variations on the name "Abegg"—"Papillons"—"Carnaval"—"Davidsbündler"—Shorter Pieces—Piece Groups—"Fantasiestücke" (Op. 12)—The Concertos—"Variation" Work.

As Madame Schumann herself infers, Schumann the musician is best viewed in his *music* itself. Commencing with the pianoforte music, this is amazing in its quantity, variety and rare excellence. Childhood, the student, the amateur, the *virtuoso* are all catered for; and to each his pabulum is given in a most acceptable and attractive fashion, can one but take the trouble of peering beneath an apparently complicated and sometimes difficult exterior for the hidden mine of wealth beneath. For the beauties of Schumann's *Clavier* music are not superficial, nor are they always disclosed upon a first reading. Like his great predecessor, to whom he himself so strongly pinned his faith, *i.e.*, J. S. Bach, Schumann requires study—earnest, deep and devoted—if we would draw the veil of his mysticism aside and taste the sweetness of the kernel that lies within the often apparently obstinate casing of the nut. Those

Piano Compositions

things which cost us most in expenditure of means, thought and trouble, once being acquired—if they have the genuine ring about them—seldom fail to win our lasting affection. So is it with the music of Bach and Schumann. Herein we want more than a facility to "sight read" in order to fully comprehend. But once having done so, we realise that to penetrate one shaft deeper into the unfathomed mine of music has disclosed richer ore than we hitherto dreamed of, and so we count the labour of extra digging light.

Music for Young People

To give a chronological summary of Schumann's pianoforte music is unnecessary. To begin with Schumann's "Child" music. By this we do not mean his own earliest compositions,[1] but those works which, even towards the close of his period of activity, he always delighted to pour forth for, and with regard to, young people. Foremost among these comes, perhaps, the famous "Album für die Jugend" (Op. 68), the artistic cover of which, as we have said, was specially arranged for by the composer with Richter, who designed it. Among these forty-three charming little pieces, "The Merry Peasant" is, doubtless, the best known. But many other numbers—gems in their own tiny and unpretentious way—might be mentioned. Such a passage as the following (from the "Volksliedchen")

[1] Wiedebein, the Brunswick song-writer, thus wrote to Schumann of some early songs submitted to him: "Your songs have many faults, some of them very many; but I should call them natural and youthful errors rather than intellectual ones. You are highly endowed by nature; profit by your gifts, and the respect of the world will not be denied you."

is sprightly and quaint for little fingers, and contains, in a nutshell, an excellent lesson in early staccato playing and phrasing. In the "Kleine Studie," beginning

we can well imagine that the composer, while inculcating *legato arpeggio* playing, was preparing the child's mind for future acquaintance with J. S. Bach's exquisite "First" Prelude from the "Well Tempered Klavier." The dainty "Mignon" and many other short fragments are also noteworthy. Among Child Music are the "Kinderscenen," an earlier work (Op. 15), in which occurs the tranquil and pleasing "Träumerei"; and the "Drei Clavier Sonaten für die Jugend" (Op. 118), which the musician specially wrote for his

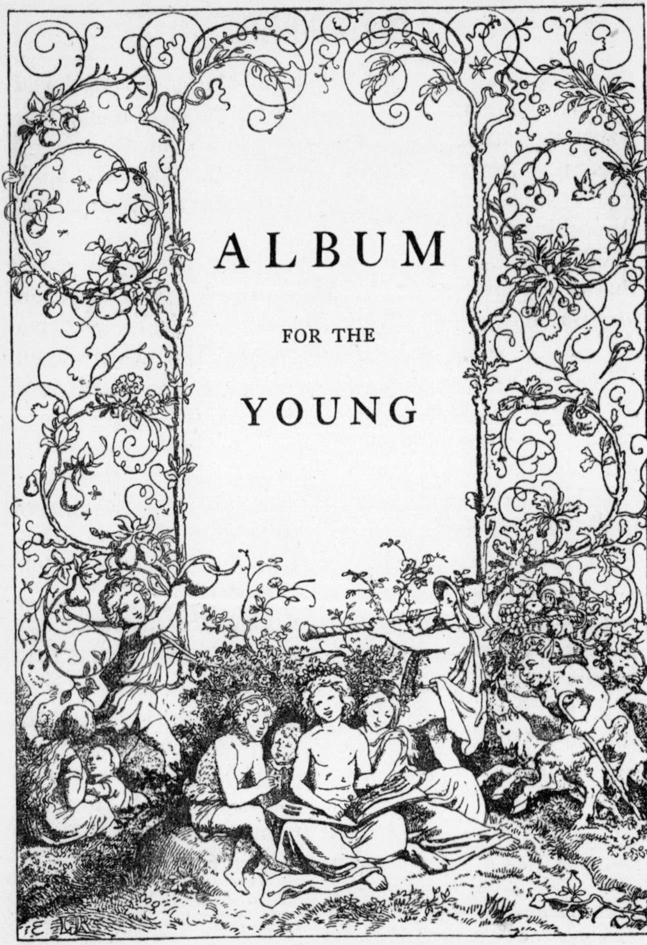

DESIGN OF TITLE-PAGE OF "ALBUM FOR THE YOUNG"

Printed by kind permission of Messrs Breitkopf & Härtel (Leipzig)

three eldest daughters, Julie, Elise and Marie. The freshness and naïvety of this Child Music is all the more remarkable when we consider the philosophic intensity of Schumann's musical genius. Yet with the children he could be a child, and this embodies one of the most charming traits of his disposition.[1]

Pianoforte Sonatas

Of regular pianoforte sonatas, Schumann wrote three, that in F ♯ minor (Op. 11), dedicated to Clara by Florestan and Eusebius; Sonate No. 2 (Op. 22), inscribed to Madame Voigt; and Grande Sonate (Op. 14), a tribute of his friendship and respect for Ignace Moscheles, from whom he had obtained his youthful inspiration.[2] Concerning these works much might be said, and the scholarship of the latter especially calls for admiration; but we must leave them to every musician's personal exploration. Many other separate items for the piano, such as the Scherzo (Op. 14), as also the Toccata (Op. 7), dedicated to his friend Louis Schunke, and apparently written under the inspiration of J. S. Bach; and the Allegro (Op. 8), composed in 1831 and inscribed to "Mdlle. la Baronne Ernestine de Fricken"—a little sketch full of daring key change, and redolent, indeed, of many modes—must be merely named in this connection. The same remark applies to much of the miscellaneous work in classical form, such as "Vier Fugen" (Op. 72), the "Vier Märsche" (Op. 76), and the "Sieben Clavierstücke in Fughettenform" (Op. 126). In these we see

[1] *See* reference to that interesting letter of the composer's in which he himself contrasts his feelings when writing the "Kinderscenen" and the "Album für die Jugend," p. 125.

[2] Page 6.

Schumann more or less under the slavery of "form" requirements. He meets his obligation with marvellous *abandon*, and adorns the dry skeleton of scholasticism with trappings all his own; but the poet-musician is happier when, as in his fantasies and purely imaginative pieces, he gives full swing to his mental imagery and power of portraiture in tone.

Variations on the Name "Abegg"

Particularly do we see Schumann unique in his powerful and original treatment of the piano when he depicts definite personalities or poetic images of places or things. Even in his Opus. 1, the theme on the name "Abegg," there is promise of a strength and musical depictment which was to reach a climax in works like the "Carnaval" and the "Davidsbündlertänze." The young lady, Fräulein Meta Abegg,[1] he had met at a ball when an impressionable student, and he thus immortalises the circumstances in tone forms:—

[1] He poetically inscribes the piece to Mademoiselle Pauline, Comtesse d'Abegg.

This was not the first time that "musical" letters in a name had furnished a tone subject. Bach had written a fugue on his own name; but Schumann was to carry the idea to a fanciful extent, never dreamt of before, in his famous "Carnaval." Preceding this had come the "Papillons" (Op. 2),[1] a series of short pieces, in which he bases the subject-matter upon a fanciful idea of a masked ball as described in Jean Paul's *Flegeljahre*. The sections in "Papillons" are little more than fragments; but they have a rare charm and a youthful sparkle of tenderness and merriment. The familiar "Grossvatertanz," an old German folk-song, is introduced with much humour and effectiveness, and the whole forms a kind of sound-picture representing the various personages in the dance, as also the talk of the lovers.

"*Papillons*"

On a still more advanced, as well as more developed, scale comes the famous "Carnaval" (Op. 9). This is based almost entirely upon the musical letters of Schumann's name, *i.e.*, S, C, H, A,[2] which, when transposed, gave A, S, C, H, the birthplace of Ernestine von Fricken, to whom the composer was for a short time betrothed. This explains the title "Sphinxes" of one of the segments; and the "letters" themselves come bounding in, boisterously and merrily, to impress themselves as *lettres dansantes* upon the listener.[3] Few but one of Schumann's imaginative nature could have conceived such a quaint and charming short panorama of sound-pictures. As the name of this composition—or

"*Carnaval*"

[1] Dedicated to Thérèse, Rosalie and Emilie.

[2] In German nomenclature, Es (Eb), C, H (B), A.

[3] Spitta (Grove).

rather series of short compositions—suggests, we might well imagine a gay *fête* where, between the pauses of the dance, we get glimpses not only of the fanciful Pierrot and Arlequin, but also of Eusebius and Florestan (various phases of the composer's own nature), Chiarina (Clara Wieck), Chopin, "Estrella," each personality depicted with a delicacy and charm which would, in a kindred art, remind one of cameo painting. Under the title "Estrella," we may or may not have a musical delineation of the fair Ernestine. It is not uninteresting to note that this episode is marked *con affetto*, whereas "Chiarina" is characterised as *passionato*. We quote a short opening passage from each :—

"CHIARINA."

"ESTRELLA."

The essentially romantic idea of the whole tone-picture, and especially its effective winding up with the vigorous and ever-quickening so-called "march" of the Davidsbündler against the Philistines, gives one a sense of something quite novel in the domain of *Clavier* music. Therein is no vulgar demonstration of "programme" billeting; yet we see in dim veiled forms, as it were, the dream visions of Schumann, the poet-musician, pass before us, with a keen appreciation of all that was pure and fair and lovable in womanhood, and a manly and joyous determination to trample under foot everything that savoured of paltriness and superficiality in his art. No one can hear the "Carnaval" well rendered by a talented performer—and it takes a truly gifted player to do it justice—and not be impressed by a feeling that therein the piano speaks a word language, tender, dreamy, and, in a way, daring, yet entirely free from mere display or even show of the virtuosity which it demands to render it adequately. The extreme difficulty to the ordinary pianist in the correct interpretation of Schumann's pianoforte music—the abnormal stretches and the requirements of neat and dainty pedalling as well as taste in the use of *tempo rubato*—has perhaps deterred many students from a closer familiarity with the works of a master that grow more enthralling the better we get in touch with them. This is a pity; but, in one way, it is better so. Mozart, Mendelssohn and even Beethoven are often mercilessly "murdered" by the mere note-mechanic. Schumann's works offer less temptation this way from the innate reason of their exclusiveness.

Preceding the "Carnaval," in date of composition, had come

the "Davidsbündlertänze" (Op. 6), a series of character sketches and phases of musical thought which deserve to be better known than they are. They consist of no less than eighteen short segments, and these, with their ever-varying rhythms and ingenious harmonic changes and combinations, may well be considered to convey many varied sentiments, among which *humour*—quaint, merry, and at times playfully mocking—is not wanting. That these movements are "dances" in the usual sense of the word can scarcely be asserted, any more than Schumann's "march" of the "Davidsbündler," which introduces the well-known "Grossvater" dance, partakes of the customary march form. Even in these matters Schumann was unconventional. He suggests a shadowy outline rather than a cut-and-dry formula. Thus is he the true poet and genius —ever moulding his materials after a pattern of his own rather than upon the models of others.

"Davidsbündlertänze"

Of short pieces of Schumann's that enjoy quite a wide popularity are some of the "Albumblätter," among which "Wiegenliedchen" and "Schlummerlied" are well-known. The "Novelletten" (Op. 21), especially that beautiful opening one in F, with its exquisite *cantabile* second part, are frequently played. The melody and flowing rhythm of these, as also their fresh chordal progressions and novel phrasing, render them particularly attractive to accomplished pianists. Among favourite numbers must also be quoted "Arabesque"—the tender flow, the varied inner sections, and the sudden key changes of which linger pleasurably in the memory of the

Shorter Pieces

hearer long after the strains have ceased to fall upon the physical ear. The dreamy mysticism, as displayed in the daring modulations which the composer is so fond of using, may be partially exemplified in a short quotation from this particular piece, especially as its context, owing to the popularity of the item itself, can be the more easily consulted by our pianist readers:—

The whole concludes with a beautiful tranquil cadence worthy of Bach.

Piece Groups

In noble piece-groups, or sound-cycles, as we might call them, Schumann the musician seems to have been most at home. The vigorous and stirring "Faschingsschwank" (Op. 26), written in his Vienna period, and dedicated to his letter-friend, Simonin de Sire,[1] may be classed under this heading. In this category is particularly to be mentioned the delightful "Waldscenen" (Op. 82), in which series occurs the weird and wonderful "Vogel als Prophet," marked by the

[1] *See* page 41.

composer *Langsam, sehr zart*[1] (Slow, and very delicately). Very few players, perhaps, truly grasp the almost ethereal, *spiritual* nature of this little fragment. It seems nearly always rendered too quickly or too heavily. Very lovely, too, are the "Nachtstücke," the first of which is of a choral character. Concerning the "Humoresken," Schumann has himself something of interest to say, for he remarks[2] that the French could not understand the term, and deplores that there is no word in their language for *Gemüthliche* (good-naturedly), and for humour. "Kreisleriana" (Op. 16) is also referred to by the composer in the same connection.[3] He mentions liking it best of any of his compositions written up to that date (1839), and again speaks of the title being only properly understood by Germans. He then describes Kreisler, as he was created in Hoffmann's novel, as "an eccentric, wild, and gifted Capellmeister."[4] The fantastic character who appears in Hoffmann's sketch blowing bubbles, with a reckless air of utter unconcern of the world and its ways, appealed strongly to Schumann; and it is not a little pathetic to note that the imaginary and the real musician had many points in common, even in the matter of the last sad catastrophe, as Hoffmann eventually represents his Capellmeister going insane.

We cannot leave the piece-groups without noticing in particular that very well-known one, the "Fantasiestücke"

[1] Be it remarked here that Schumann prefers to attach musical expression indications by German words, to the almost complete exclusion of the usual Italian terms.

[2] Letter to Simonin de Sire, Vienna, March 15, 1839. *See* also page 41.

[3] *Ibid.* [4] *Ibid.*

(Op. 12). One of the sections, though but a mere fragment, "Warum?" (Why?) has become deservedly popular. It is full of a tender, passionate melodiousness which grows upon one with closer familiarity. The first movement, "Des Abends," is also particularly beautiful. It reminds one of the fall of a mellow and tranquil twilight—the time of musing and sweet memories. "Aufschwung," which follows, is a complete contrast to the two segments just named. It is full of life, subtle aspiration, and a kind of exultant joy coupled to tender solicitude—an ecstatic soul-song of gladness and triumph. "Traumes Wirren" is a dainty and exquisite fragment; but requires, for its adequate rendering, a particularly facile and finished technique. It might almost be called a fairy-piece—so light is it, airy as a dream, and full of a delicate and fantastic imagery which baffles description. Other portions are the beautiful "In der Nacht," "Fabel," and "Ende vom Lied." Nor should we forget "Grillen," with its quaint, humorous touches, not unmixed with a slight pathos. How striking, for example, is the following passage from this fragment:—

"*Fantasie-stücke*" (*Op.* 12)

FROM "GRILLEN."

What energy, exhilaration, and yet a touch of yearning is here! The student is especially directed to note the strong climax at (*a*), the syncopations at (*b*) and (*b*¹), and the "free" resolution of the dominant 13th at (*c*), giving the pathetic glamour just alluded to.

The Concertos

Among works for the pianoforte may also be included the masterly Concertos for that instrument and orchestra. Opus 54, dedicated to Ferdinand Hiller, is a fine work of this class. In it, as might be expected, the pianoforte plays by no means a secondary part in the *ensemble;* yet the orchestra is treated with a power and intensity of colouring which heightens rather than eclipses the importance of the solo instrument. Other works of this kind were the "Concert-stück" for pianoforte and orchestra (Op. 92), written in that fruitful year 1849, almost the last, alas! of creative productiveness; and the "Concert-Allegro" (Op. 134) composed for J. Brahms as late as 1853. While on the subject of Concertos it is worthy of note that Schumann has bequeathed to musical literature Concertos for violin and for 'cello—both with orchestra—as also a remarkable work for four horns and orchestra (Op. 86).

But it is manifestly impossible, amid such an *embarras de richesse*, to speak of all that Schumann did for his favourite instrument. One department, however, calls for a passing notice. Most of the great musicians tried their hand at Variations on a given theme. In fact, that form of composition is, in a way, the basis of the creative musician's art, and is the stepping-stone to, as the highest development of, the best thematic work. Doubtless the "Etudes Symphoniques" are the most important instances of Schumann's scholarship in this department. In the treatment of Variations, as in all other work, he was original, and showed how little influence his predecessors' or contemporaries' methods really had upon him. He brings out the resources of the pianoforte in ways scarcely dreamt of before and hardly rivalled since. Nor, under his pen, is the Variation ever trivial or a mere volley of fireworks. Display of any kind, indeed, he strenuously avoids. Yet in harmonic treatment, rhythm and speed we are constantly reminded of the diversity in which one dominant idea can be presented to us. Once more, in this branch of his work, the many-sidedness of Schumann's genius shows itself. Variations seem to have attracted him from the first. We have already referred to Opus 1, the Theme with Variations on the name "Abegg." There is also to be noted the "Etudes," written after hearing Paganini play (Op. 3 and Op. 10), and especially the "Impromptus" on a theme of Clara Wieck (Op. 5), which, as it would doubtless interest our readers, we venture to quote herewith :—

"Variation" Work

The above is highly interesting and suggestive. There is a certain earnestness and energy about the melody itself which is, in no small degree, characteristic of its composer. For the able way in which Schumann treated this theme in Variation form the reader is recommended to a personal study of the Opus 5 in question.

CHAPTER XVII

Compositions in all Forms—Symphonies—Overtures—Chamber Music —"Paradise and the Peri"—The Choral Ballads, etc.—Wanted, an Ideal Grand Opera—"Genoveva" brought out under Difficulties—Faith of the Composer in his Work—A Plea for the Libretto—Has "Genoveva" had a Fair Hearing?—The "Genoveva" Music.

Compositions in all Forms

WE have lingered over the pianoforte compositions of Schumann, because in them, more than in any other department of his art—if perhaps we except his Songs—the composer appeals to the widest circle of listeners. This is only natural, as his own training was, at first, directed altogether toward that wonderful domestic instrument.

The importance and value of Schumann's work in other branches of musical art cannot be dismissed summarily. His skill is orchestral colouring, considering that he played no orchestral instrument; the excellent specimens of his chamber music; and the fact that, with an almost abnormal power of scope, he tried his powers at cantata, opera and oratorio form—all these points call for our reverent attention and sincerest admiration of his fertility in output, as the immense expenditure of inventive thought and unceasing exertion which the vast and varied full catalogues of his musical works display.

Concerning Schumann's Symphonies, with Dr Spitta's able estimate, in Grove's *Dictionary*, that these works are unquestionably the nearest of all to the "Immortal Nine" of Beethoven, the connoisseur will readily agree.

Symphonies

That in B flat, the first, is very fresh and bright, and vividly brings, as the composer intended it should, the image of the fair but fleeting Spring before us. This was written at the zenith of his activity and happiness, in 1841, one year after his marriage. The D minor Symphony also belongs to this year, and by many it is considered an advance in intensity and scholarship upon the first. In that fine work for orchestra which is composed of Overture, Scherzo, and Finale, and is often called Schumann's Third Symphony, we have an example of a Scherzo which, for striking originality, is worthy of being placed side by side with the similar masterpieces of Beethoven. Musical humour wonderfully affected both these great minds; and none have, it may be, before or since, better emphasised the musical "joke" than they. The C major Symphony is more in classical style than any of the others. Schumann himself says[1] that it was written when he was recovering from the serious illness of 1845, and hence he accounts for the "sorrowful music" of the melancholy Adagio in which the bassoon is so ably treated. In the E flat Symphony, generally known as the "Rhenish" (Op. 97), the composer gives full play to his fancy for scene depicting. Herein we are bade to imagine a great Festival at Cologne, with its attending ceremonies, such as the installation of the Archbishop, etc. The themes in the

[1] Letter, April 22, 1849, to D. C. Otten, Musik Director at Hamburg.

opening movement of this fine work are well contrasted, and the development is novel and effective. The scoring of the "Intermezzo" is particularly beautiful. Those who have heard the work performed cannot fail to remember the melodious phrase on the 'celli, the *cantabile* passages for horns, and the telling *staccato* accompaniment on strings and wood. The whole has been compared to "a pleasant trip on the Rhine at sunset."[1] Then follows that delicious "Andante" in A flat, the impressive slow movement in E flat, and lastly the strong, vividly-coloured "Finale" which brings the work to a striking close.

Overtures

Next to the Symphonies might be mentioned the Overtures. Among these, that to the opera "Genoveva" is a wonderful piece of orchestral colouring—an epitome in tone of the tale that follows, wherein the composer treats of true love as opposed to baulked passion, with the attendant episodes of murderous jealousy, treachery, and the final triumph of virtue and faith. The Overture to "Manfred" is also a striking example of instrumentation, suggesting a keen mental struggle, and full of the tragic intensity of Byron's morbid poem. Mostcritics consider the "Faust" Overture as scarcely commensurate with the significance of Goethe's famous tragedy. Other compositions in this form, issuing from Schumann's wondrously prolific pen, are the "Braut von Messina," "Hermann und Dorothea," and the "Rheinweinlied" Overtures—the latter of which, in particular, forms a very attractive concert piece.

In writing Chamber Music, probably as he played no

[1] Louis Kelterbarn.

member of the "quartet of strings," Schumann treated his melodic phrases generally from a pianist's point of view. For all this, his three string quartets are works full of originality and charm. Most musicians are familiar with his beautiful "Quintet for Strings and Pianoforte" (Op. 44), a work which, even upon a first hearing, impresses one with its fervour and rich harmonic structure. Wasielewski[1] considers it as the tone picture of a wanderer or mountaineer climbing ever higher and higher till the glorious prospect of a fair landscape bursts upon one's view from the highest summit. Hence we might apply to the Quintet the term which Longfellow has immortalised in his well-known poem, "Excelsior." No better estimate of Schumann's Chamber Music can be mentioned than that of Dr Spitta in his article on the composer's works in Grove's *Dictionary*. To this the student is referred, and the best known of the string quartets, Op. 47, is recommended as being well worth a careful analysis.

Chamber Music

We pass now to a necessarily limited survey of Schumann's larger choral works (with orchestral accompaniment). Pre-eminently among these stands "Paradise and the Peri," a composition which has not obtained the recognition which it deserves. Described as a *profane oratorio*, it can, in reality, be classed neither as cantata, opera or oratorio. It occupies a unique position among works of this kind, and is best understood as the musical reflex of Moore's imaginative and fascinating poem on a semi-

"Paradise and the Peri"

[1] *Life of Schumann.*

mythical, semi-sacred topic, the whole being embellished with the rich glow of the East, while underlying all are the universal emotions of patriotism, self-sacrificing love, and the dying sinner's repentance. Albeit the choral and vocal parts generally of the "Peri" have been criticised from the performer's aspect of adequate effect produced, the score itself discloses only beauties of the highest order. The Peri's solo music throughout, if sung at the lowered (A=439) pitch, is redolent with grace, charm and appropriateness; nor can the dramatic soprano desire a more telling number, with its fine cadential climax, than "Rejected" and the aria which follows. The "Chorus of Houris" is a poem within a poem. Now nearer, now further away, are wafted to us the singing of the happy spirits; and through the rifts in the clouds we seem to get glimpses of a Land where all is calm peace and unalloyed joy. Even the *pianissimo* concluding bars seem but the gentle dropping of the veil over a beatific vision; and those who trouble to penetrate the poet-musician's meaning are much more impressed by a *diminuendo* treatment than they would be by the final crashing of loud dominant and tonic cadence chords. To enter fully into the rare attractiveness of such tone painting, one should examine the score, and then hear the work well and sympathetically performed.

More than one able critic has given an erudite verdict upon the Choral Ballads (a style of composition which seems to have strongly attracted Schumann). Possibly the texts of these scarcely lend themselves to lyrical musical treatment. The weakly sentimentalism of the libretto of "The Pilgrimage of the Rose" had also, doubtless, its effect upon the music. The wonder of the "Faust" music, as a kind of tone-elucidation of Goethe's immortal text, is perhaps only fully appreciable to the German mind, to which the poem is as an Heroic of the people. Among shorter compositions for chorus it may be that Schumann's settings of Hebbel's "Nachtlied" (Op. 108), and especially the beautiful "Requiem for Mignon" (from "Wilhelm Meister"), carry off the palm. The "Requiem" seems to us a choral gem of subtle and delicate charm. Short portions for solo voices are most effectively and judiciously introduced, and the orchestration possesses a certain weird exquisiteness which cannot fail to enhance the poetry of the text. All who have heard this little work well rendered will remember the *pianissimo* opening for oboes, bassoons and horns, as the effective introduction of the harp in the score.

The Choral Ballads, etc.

Grand Opera is generally the crowning ambition of the composer; but few, indeed, are they who achieve therein a lasting or wholly satisfying success. Many causes militate against the production of the *perfect* opera. Text and music are often ill-assorted; scenic and dramatic requirements are overlooked by the musician; the claims of the Divine Art are frequently made subservient to the vanity of singers or the mere mechanical notions of stage accessory. If an acting manager existed who was a poet and creative musician as well as a man of unlimited means, energy and ambition, we might look for a Grand Opera which would leave the critics nothing to cavil at; but such a combination did not exist even in Mozart, still

Wanted, an Ideal Grand Opera

less in Wagner. That sensitive, highly-strung Schumann could have succeeded where even the giant Handel notably failed, was scarcely to be expected. In no way, however, is the multi-sidedness of Schumann's genius shown than in his treatment of the *dramma per musica*.

"Genoveva" brought out under Difficulties

Some enterprises seem fettered from their conception and are only carried through by sheer force of their originator. This was remarkably the case with "Genoveva." When the story tardily presented itself, neither its author Hebbel nor the poet Reinick gave the musician much assistance in arranging an opera book; and finally Schumann became his own librettist. When, at length, the musical score was complete, procrastinations and difficulties of all kinds delayed its production. The performance, finally, fell at that period of the year when audiences prefer to be in the open air to the close atmosphere of a theatre. The more fully to seal the fate of "Genoveva," the greatest critics, with perhaps the one exception of Spohr, have since been unanimous in condemning both text and music—the one as cutting out all the strongest situations of Hebbel's and Tieck's tragedy; the other as deficient in supporting the dramatic situation, and altogether inadequate to convey a satisfactory or pleasurable impression.

In view of so much opposition, it is significant that Schumann himself never lost faith in his "Genoveva"; and, even in the face of an apparently unanimous opinion in the other direction on the part of connoisseurs and the public, he maintained to the end that every phrase of the work was fraught with dramatic meaning. This was not through mere egotism or obstinacy—no musician was freer from these traits than Schumann. What if the inner sense of the seer saw what others of more material mind saw not? What if the tone poet, who chose a subject only after years of thought, and whose libretto requirements even the foremost versifiers of the day could not satisfy, knew infinitely better than his would-be critics and advisers what was or was not fitting in the great sound-poem to which his genius gave birth?

Faith of the Composer in his Work

Upon a careful reading, the libretto of "Genoveva" strikes one as being coherent, interesting and notably strong in character delineation—a trait we do not often find in opera books. As to the omissions of the "hind" and the "child," which have been much animadverted upon by commentators, where Schumann was striving to maintain the one dominant idea, *i.e.*, the ultimate triumph of virtuous love—such matters are trivial side-lights which he probably showed mature judgment in discarding. The episode of the faithful retainer, Drago, being accredited with amorous intentions towards his liege lord's young wife, is no more incredulous than many other incongruities which we are bade believe in fiction, and which constantly confront us in daily life. If the story seems "hurried" in places, more praise than blame may be given to the narrator on this account. The majority of operatic *scenæ* are dragged out to an inordinate length, nor is great Wagner himself the least sinner in this respect. The jealous husband, who leaves his young wife to the care of

A Plea for the Libretto

a man of his own years, and who, upon a written rumour of her unfaithfulness, ruthlessly commands her to be handed over to the assassin, his murderous ire turning to repentant love-making when he discovers that his almost victim is innocent, commands neither our honour nor regard; and probably Schumann did not mean to make a hero of his Siegfried. Indeed, as the title of the work suggests, "Genoveva," the shrinking yet dauntless woman who, in the hour of danger, can save herself by a well-directed scornful word—as later on, from the death-dealing sword, by prayer—is a creature around whom the entire interest of the drama centres, and at the close we could wish her a better spouse. It is, moreover, worthy of note that Schumann, like Shakespeare, does not make his villains *utterly* bad.[1] Thus Golo has his many qualms of conscience, and at times we are more inclined to pity than to blame him. Even Margaret, the wicked witch, regrets that she ever let the angel-child of tenderness and sympathy depart from her in youth. There is a power in little touches of this kind which would reclaim any work from reproach.

Has "Genoveva" had a Fair Hearing?

Indeed, where the reproach in the case of Schumann's work comes in we scarcely see, save that it lies in the fact that it has not yet had a fair chance of wide and repeated hearings to enable one to judge of its manifold beauties. That it would be "popular" in the sense of furnishing tunes to the humming and whistling fraternity we can scarcely maintain; but no more do we look for this element in the other works of Schumann. Like his great model, J. S.

[1] The *Iago* ("Othello") of Shakespeare perhaps alone excepted.

Bach, Schumann is essentially the "musician's musician"; and, as such, he must also be classed as an opera composer.

Of the many musical beauties of "Genoveva" we may mention the tasteful *melos* or *arioso* which, throughout, takes the place of recitative—another matter of erudite condemnation which resents anything outside stereotypism; the strong soprano *rôle* of Genoveva—notably her sacred solo, "O Thou, Whose ever watchful care"; such duos as "If but a bird were I"; and the chorus work, and notably the overture—all dainty, appropriate, and tinged with a fine poetic imagery which only needs closer acquaintance to endear it to the hearer.

We have said enough—more than our space limitations warrant—on the subject of Schumann's one opera, "Genoveva," and it only remains to hope that theatrical *impressarii* will once more turn their attention to this worthy score; it certainly appears to us as "*Genoveva*" much more deserving of public notice than *Music* many highly-vaunted modern successors. The allegations that it is dry and monotonous can only be disproved by the *vox populi*. We cannot better conclude our notice of it than by quoting the opening of a bright little chorus which precedes the Finale.

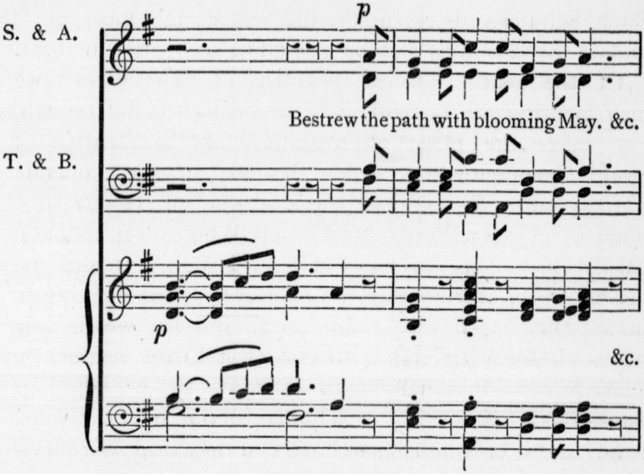
S. & A.
p
Bestrew the path with blooming May. &c.
T. & B.
p
&c.

The entire chorus should, of course, be examined in order to appreciate its tenderness and naïvety. From the few bars given it will, however, be evident that, in musical form at all events, the construction is neither obscure nor repellent. In concluding, we would reiterate that "Genoveva" deserves at least a fair hearing.

CHAPTER XVIII

Sacred Music—Well-known Songs—Other Vocal Favourites—Poetic Numbers—Love Songs—Nature of the Song Music—Artistic Accompaniments—Concluding Remarks.

So many able notices of the "Faust" as of the "Manfred" music have been written [1] that it appears superfluous on our part to add further. It is curious to note that, towards the close of his career, Schumann turned his attention to sacred music. In this he resembled many great composers; witness Handel's and Haydn's oratorios, as indeed the similar famous works of Mendelssohn and Gounod, composed within view, one might say, of their "passing." Writing to one Strackerjan, an Oldenburg officer, Schumann remarks that "a musician's highest aim is to apply his power to religious music." [2]

Sacred Music

The "Mass," as the "Requiem" (known as Op. 147 and Op. 148 respectively), were specially composed for Düsseldorf, and were in reality his "swan songs." Even among the strict Church forms he introduced an original number. His poetic reverence for the Madonna comes out in the Mass in the form of an Offertory, "Tota pulchra

[1] *See* references in Wasielewski's, as in Reissmann's, *Life;* also Spitta's article, "Schumann," *Dictionary of Music and Musicians* (Grove).

[2] Letter, dated January 13, 1851.

es, Maria." One is reminded also, in this connection, of his beautiful song in the "Dichterliebe" (The Poet's Love) cycle, in which he has set Heine's exquisite poem beginning, "Im Rhein im heiligen Strome," wherein the Virgin's picture in the Cologne Cathedral reminds the poet of his best beloved.[1] That Schumann, as Mozart, should each have written a "Requiem" when entering the Valley of the Shadow, has a strange and pathetic coincidence about it. We have already spoken of the profane oratorio, "Paradise and the Peri." Schumann himself seems to have been seriously interested in his scholarly setting of Rückert's "Advent Hymn."

Well-known Songs

Last, but not least, among the Schumann compositions which our space permits us to notice, come the Songs, most of which were composed in that, probably, most blissful year of his life, 1840-1841, when his happy marriage with Clara Wieck put an end to a long period of struggle and uncertainty. Perhaps no Schumann numbers, after a small group of his better-known pianoforte pieces, are so widely appreciated as the songs, "Ich Grolle Nicht" (I will not grieve) and "The Two Grenadiers." In the former we see intense passion — at once exultant and despairing—and the closing climax makes this item particularly acceptable to vocalists, albeit a touch of morbidity is not wanting. The fine rousing song of the "Grenadiers" is very popular with our best baritone vocalists, and the masterly introduction of the "Marsellaise"—a tune to which

[1] See "Dichterliebe" (English version by Lady Macfarren) in the *Schumann Song Series*, published by Novello.

Schumann was particularly partial—never fails to stir a mixed audience when well rendered.

Other Vocal Favourites

Other favourite songs[1] include "Widmung" (Devotion), in which Schumann indulges in that pet key-change of his, *i.e.*, from A flat to E. "Der Nussbaum" (The Almond Tree) is short but very dainty, no small portion of its charm lying in the flowing *arpeggio* accompaniment, the following scrap from which will give a fair idea of its nature:—

Poetic Numbers

The dreamy, poetic spirit of the composer is particularly seen in his short setting of Heine's "Lotusblume" and Byron's "My Soul is Dark." Essentially German—full of devotion to and calm pride in Fatherland—is "A Holiday on the Rhine," which, in its reiterated accompaniment, gives quite a wonderful idea of the placid flow of the river and the onward progress of the boat. The lovely "Abendlied," with its organ-like accompaniment and wonderful tranquil-

[1] For all songs quoted *see* "Schumann's Songs" in the *Royal Song Book Series*.

lity not unmixed with pathos, is too well known to need comment. An indescribable exquisiteness characterises "Mondlicht" (Moonlight), while a touch of almost hopeless sadness broods over "Zwielicht" (Twilight). "Er, der Herrlichste von allen" (usually known as Humility) is eminently vocal; and the same remark applies to the simple and touching "Aus alten Märchen" (Old Stories). Nor does Schumann always write in solemn strains; witness the sprightly little song, "Die Rose, die Lilie" (The Rose and the Lily), and many others.

Love Songs

All the musician's Love Songs, separate and in cycle form, are delicate, refined and dainty, yet by no means wanting in manly fervour and devotion. This is especially the case in his setting of the love poems of his own countrymen. In the Burns ditties, notably "My Heart is sair," we feel that Schumann was less at home. The childlike exuberance of the Gael, now rising, now falling in sunlight and shadow, is really untranslatable save in Keltic Folk Song. The difference between a Teuton and Milesian love rhapsody may best be described by instancing the contrasted feelings that are awakened by the singing of nightingale and skylark. The one is a songstress within the leafy thicket when night and moonlight make the soul pensive; the other is the hidden music of mysterious cloudland, which is heard only in perfection in the early summer morning or in the full glow of noontide sunshine. For the true understanding and appreciation of either, one needs to partake of the mental attitudes inseparable respectively from the dweller in lowlands and upon the heights.

FACSIMILE OF SCORING (FROM THE B FLAT SYMPHONY).

The "flow" of Schumann's vocal music has often been criticised. He certainly did not write for the "flashy" concert vocalist, nor yet for the *bravura* prima donna.

Nature of the Song Music

Nevertheless, if fair trouble is taken to master difficult passages, there is nothing really unsingable about his music. On the contrary, as in the piano, so in the voice; the composer depends more upon his effects obtained in *the medium range* rather than by deep drum rolls and ethereal fireworks on the keyboard, and low growls or piercing shrieks from the human throat. Schumann was too much in earnest to fetter himself by the fashion of his own or any time.

Artistic Accompaniments

The accompaniments of Schumann's songs, as might be expected from his intimate knowledge of the pianoforte, are works of art in themselves. At times, indeed, one feels that therein, rather than in the melody, we see the composer in his happiest mode as a tone painter. His methods are well worth the student's analysis; and in the rendering of his song music the good accompanist appears to claim quite as full a share of honour as the solo vocalist. Though the quoting of a single short excerpt can give but the most stunted idea of the variety and ingenuity of devices which Schumann handles with such skill in accompaniment writing, yet we cannot well leave this interesting department of his work without giving at least one instance of his musicianship in this branch. The following are the closing bars (exclusive of the final symphony, by no means an unimportant part of any of the songs) from the composer's "Ich Wand're Nicht" (usually known as "The Pleasures of Home"):—

Herein is vocal fervour, simplicity, and yet consummate artistic design in support and instrumental colouring. It is worthy of mark that the high note is introduced not for effect so much as to enhance the enthusiasm of the implied sentiment. It is needless to add that the song will best be enjoyed and appreciated in its entirety.

Concluding Remarks

Our brief survey of the compositions of Schumann does not include much of his miscellaneous work, such as the vocal and pianoforte duets,[1] part songs, etc. These will be found in Appendix A, in the list of compositions arranged according to Opus number.

The obscurity of the musician has been alleged by those who, perhaps, took not the trouble to look beneath the surface. Once more, like his revered predecessor, Bach, Schumann was ahead of his times. His work represents, in truth, a step forward in the onward march of poetic musicianship—"An essential link," as Reissmann puts it, "in the history of the general development both of culture and of art." To comprehend this great creative artist properly, one must, as has been frequently hinted, understand the man himself—his early environment, his poetic temperament, his literary tastes and aptitude, and his rare gifts of tone imagery and originality in musical output. We cannot help feeling with Wasielewski that, in the composer's songs especially, we see the *individuality* of the man, both as mortal and musician: and in the vast variety of these we can best grasp that "myriad-mindedness" of his which brings Coleridge's Shakespeare before our eyes. Wasielewski's opinion on this point seems apt in this connection. Speaking of Schumann's songs,

[1] "The Twelve Pianoforte Duets" (Op. 85), for players of all ages, are well worth the attention of students and teachers. In this collection occurs an arrangement of "Abendlied," the melody alone being given to the right-hand player.

that able biographer says that they are, "in every respect, the true children of his mind. They reveal the whole inner man, with all his lights and shades. We here find, in singular accord, depth and warmth of nature, enthusiastic feeling, fanciful deep conception, ingenious and poetic wealth of expression, and a very happy characterisation, even in the smallest details, and especially developed in the pianoforte accompaniment."[1]

Over the grave of Robert Schumann, in the Bonn churchyard, is the superb monument executed by Donndorf and erected in the composer's memory through the appreciation of a wide circle of his eminent friends and admirers. A still greater monument—and one doubtless more imperishable than stone—exists in his works. His essays—as well as his music—grow upon us with closer acquaintance; nor can we think that the present generation has, as yet, grasped their rich meaning and significance. To a study of these living emblems of one who has passed from sensual vision, we commend student as professor. Therein is the output of the genius of a great tone poet worthy of our highest reverence and admiration. Therein music and poetry immortalise the man who, though he be dead, yet speaketh.

[1] Wasielewski's *Life of Schumann.*

Appendix A

CATALOGUE OF SCHUMANN'S PUBLISHED COMPOSITIONS.

(*Arranged according to Opus Number.*)

Opus

1. Variations for Pianoforte on the name "Abegg."
2. Papillons (12 short pieces).
3. Studies after Paganini's Caprices.
4. Intermezzi (2 books).
5. Impromptus (Variations on Clara Wieck's theme)
6. Davidsbündlertänze (18 numbers)
7. Toccata.
8. Allegro.
9. Carnival (21 pieces).
10. Second Set of Studies after Paganini's Caprices.
11. Sonata in F sharp minor.
12. Fantasiestücke (8 pieces).
13. Études Symphoniques.
14. Sonata in F minor.
15. Kinderscenen (13 pieces).
16. Kreisleriana (8 pieces).
17. Fantasia.
18. Arabeske.
19. Blumenstück.
20. Humoreske.
21. Novelletten (4 books).
22. Sonata in G minor.
23. Nachtstücke.

Schumann

Opus

24. Liederkreis (9 songs by Heine).
25. Myrthen (26 songs).
26. Faschingsschwank aus Wien (pf.).
27. Lieder und Gesänge (5 songs).
28. Drei Romanzen (pf.).
29. Setting of Three Poems by Geibel, for small chorus, triangle, and tambourines *ad lib.* (choral).
30. Setting of Three Poems by Geibel.
31. Setting of Three Song Poems by Chamisso.
32. Four Pianoforte Pieces (Scherzo, Gigue, Romanze, and Fughette).
33. Six Four-Part Songs (for male voices).
34. Four Duets for Soprano and Tenor.
35. Setting of 12 Poems by Justinus Kerner.
36. „ „ 6 Poems by Reinick.
37. „ „ 12 Poems from Rückert's "Liebesfrühling" (Nos. 2, 4 and 11 by Clara Wieck).
38. Symphony in B flat.
39. Liederkreis (12 poems by Eichendorff).
40. Five Songs.
41. Three Quartets (for 2 violins, viola, and 'cello).
42. Song Cycle, "Frauen-Liebe und Leben."
43. Three Two-Part Songs.
44. Quintet for Pianoforte, 2 violins, viola, and 'cello.
45. Romanzen und Balladen (vocal).
46. Andante and Variations (duet for 2 pfs.).
47. Quartet for pf., violin, viola, and 'cello.
48. Song Cycle, "Dichterliebe."
49. Romanzen und Balladen.
50. Paradise and the Peri (oratorio).
51. Lieder und Gesänge
52. Overture, Scherzo, and Finale (orchestra).
53. Romanzen und Balladen (vocal).
54. Concerto for pf. and orchestra (A minor).
55. Songs by Burns (for mixed chorus).
56. Studies for Pedal Piano (6 pieces in canon form).
57. Belsatzar (Ballad by Heine).
58. Sketches for Pedal Piano.
59. Four Songs for mixed chorus.

Appendix A

Opus

60. Six Fugues on the name Bach (pf.).
61. Symphony in C major.
62. Three Songs for male voices.
63. Trio for pf., violin, and 'cello (D minor).
64. Romanzen und Balladen (vocal).
65. Ritonelle (for male voices in canon form).
66. Bilder aus Osten (pf. duets).
67. Romanzen und Balladen (for chorus).
68. Album for the Young (43 short pf. pieces).
69. Romances for female voices (pf. accompaniment *ad lib.*).
70. Adagio and Allegro for pf. and horn ('cello or violin *ad lib.*).
71. Adventlied (poem by Rückert).
72. Four Fugues (pf.).
73. Fantasiestücke for pf. and clarinet (violin or 'cello *ad lib.*).
74. Song Cycle, "Spanisches Liederspiel" (vocal and choral).
75. Romanzen und Balladen (for chorus).
76. Four Marches.
77. Lieder und Gesänge.
78. Four Duets for Soprano and Tenor.
79. Album of Songs for the Young.
80. Trio for pf., violin, and 'cello.
81. Genoveva (opera in 4 acts).
82. Waldscenen (pf.).
83. Three Songs.
84. A Parting Song.
85. Twelve Clavierstücke (pf. duets).
86. Concertstück (for 4 horns and orchestra).
87. Der Handschuh (Ballad by Schiller).
88. Phantasiestücke for pf., violin, and 'cello.
89. Six Songs by Willfried von der Neun.
90. Setting of 6 poems by Lenau, and Requiem.
91. Romances for female voices.
92. Concertstücke for pf. and orchestra.
93. Versweifle nicht im Schmerzensthal (motet for double male voice choir).
94. Three Romances for pf. and oboe (violin or 'cello *ad lib*).

Opus
95. Three Songs from Byron's Hebrew Melodies (harp or pf. accompaniment).
96. Lieder und Gesänge (vocal).
97. Symphony in E flat.
98*a*. Lieder und Gesänge (from Goethe's "Wilhelm Meister.")
98*b*. Requiem for Mignon (from Goethe's "Wilhelm Meister.")
99. Bunte Blätter.
100. Overture to Schiller's "Braut von Messina."
101. Minnespiel (from Rückert's "Liebesfruhling.")
102. Five Pieces for pf. and 'cello.
103. Mädchenlieder (by Elizabeth Kulmann).
104. Seven Songs (by Elizabeth Kulmann).
105. Sonata for pf. and violin.
106. Schön Hedwig (Ballad by Hebbel).
107. Six Songs.
108. Nachtlied (by Hebbel).
109. Ballscenen (pf. duets).
110. Trio for pf., violin, and 'cello.
111. Three Fantasiestücke.
112. The Pilgrimage of the Rose.
113. Märchenbilder (for pf. and viola—violin *ad lib.*).
114. Three Songs for three female voices.
115. Music to Byron's "Manfred."
116. Der Königssohn (Ballad by Uhland).
117. Four Husarenlieder (by Lenau.)
118. Three Pf. Sonatas for the Young.
119. Three Poems from the "Wildlieder" of Pfarrius (vocal).
120. Symphony in D minor.
121. Sonata for pf. and violin.
122. (No. 1) Ballade vom Haideknabe (Hebbel).
122. (No. 2) Die Flüchtlinge (Ballad by Shelley).
123. Rheinweinlied (Festival Overture with chorus).
124. Albumblätter (pf.).
125. Funf heitere Gesänge.
126. Seven Pieces in fughetta form.
127. Lieder und Gesänge.
128. Overture to Shakespeare's "Julius Cæsar."
129. Concerto for 'cello and orchestra.
130. Kinderball (pf. duets).

Appendix A

Opus

131. Phantasie for violin and orchestra.
132. Marchenzälungen (for pf., clarinet, and viola—violin *ad lib.*).
133. Gesänge der Frühe (pf.).
134. Concert-Allegro with Introduction (for pf. and orchestra).
135. Gedichte der Königen Maria Stuart (vocal).
136. Overture to Goethe's "Hermann und Dorothea."
137. Five Hunting Songs (for male chorus).
138. Spanische Liebeslieder.
139. Des Sängers Fluch (Ballad after Uhland).
140. Vom Pagen und der Königstochter (4 Ballads by Geibel).
141. Four Songs for Double Chorus.
142. Four Songs.
143. Der Glück von Edenhall (Ballad by Uhland).
144. New Year's Song (Rückert).
145. Romanzen und Balladen (for chorus).
146. Ditto.
147. Mass.
148. Requiem.

(*Without Opus Number, or Parts Published separately*).

Scenes from Goethe's "Faust."
Der Deutsche Rhein, patriotic song by N. Becker (with chorus).
Introduction and Allegro Appassionato (Concerto).
Overtures to "Genoveva," "Manfred," and "Faust."
Pf. Accompaniments to Bach's Suites and Sonatas for violin solo (Leipzig, Breïtkopf & Härtel).
Scherzo (pf.), originally with F minor Sonata (Op. 14).
Presto Passionato, originally with G minor Sonata (Op. 22).

Appendix B

BIBLIOGRAPHY

Robert A. Schumann's "Gesammelte Schriften über Musik und Musiker." English version—"Music and Musicians," translated, edited and annotated by Fanny Raymond Ritter.

—— "Musikalische Haus—und Lebensregelm." English version—"Advice to Young Musicians," translated by H. H. Pierson.

—— "Briefe," edited by F. G. Jansen. English version—"The Life of Robert Schumann told in his Letters," with preface by F. G. Jansen, translated by May Herbert.

—— "Jugendbriefe," edited by Madame Clara Schumann. English version—"Early Letters of Robert Schumann," translated by May Herbert.

Neue Zeitschrift für Musik (edited by Robert Schumann).

BIOGRAPHIES—

By J. A. Fuller Maitland (in the "Great Musicians" series); Hadow; A. Niggli; H. Reimann; A. Reissmann ("The Life and Works of Robert Schumann," translated by A. L. Alger); J. W. von Wasielewski; Frederick J. Crowest (in "The Great Tone Poets") etc.

Biographical sketch of Schumann in Grove's *Dictionary of Music and Musicians*, by P. Spitta.

"Die Davidsbündler; aus Robert Schumann's Sturm und Drange Periode," by F. G. Jansen.

MISCELLANEOUS—

Ambros (A. W.)—"Robert Schumann's Tage und Werke" (in *Culturhistorichen Bilder aus dem Musikleben der Gegenwart*).

Appendix B

MISCELLANEOUS—*Continued.*

Bagge—"Robert Schumann und seine Faust scenen."
David—"Les Mendelssohn-Bartholdy et Robert Schumann."
Hueffer (F.)—"Die Poesie in Der Musik."
Imbert—"Faust, par Robert Schumann."
Kalbeck (Max)—"Robert Schumann in Wien" (in *Weiner Allgemeine Zeitung*).
Laurencin (Count F. P.)—"Das Paradies und die Peri."
Lohmann—"Ueber Robert Schumann's Faust Musik."
Mesnard—"Un successeur de Beethoven" (Étude sur Robert Schumann).
Pohl (R.)—"Erinnerungen au Robert Schumann."
Vogel (B.)—"Robert Schumann's Klaviertonpoesie."
Waldersee (Count P.)—"Robert Schumann's Manfred."

Historical and critical articles in magazines, in Series of Musical Biographies, etc., etc.

Index

Index

Index

Index

THE END

Colston & Coy. Limited, Printers, Edinburgh.